G. Potts FBCV '95

Companion/Ministry; 14
Bible; 21
Peace/Crisis/Trials; 61
Goals; 71
Stress; 73
Discipleship/Stress; 74-75
Discipleship; 76
Evangelism; 78
Flexibility; 79
Men/Women; 94
Stewardship; 111
Stewardship; 111-12
Work/Ministry; 116-17
Work/Success/Stress; 119
Fatigue/Stress/Rest; 153-155
Jesus/Name; 173-74
God/Trials; 175
Church/Trials; 177
Christian Life; 191
Potential/Self-Esteem; 211
Jesus/Children/Salvation; 211
Jesus; 222

Battle FATIGUE

Are you **constantly** in a hurry?
TIRED all the time?
Overwhelmed by *"little things"*?
Always a **week away** from **being**
caught up? **Then** *you've* **got...**

Battle Fatigue

JOE B. BROWN

Nashville, Tennessee

Printed in the United States of America

Published by
Broadman & Holman Publishers
Nashville, Tennessee

Book Design: Steven Boyd

4261-54
0-8054-6154-X

Dewey Decimal Classification: 248.4
Subject Heading: STRESS (PSYCHOLOGY)
Library of Congress Card Catalog Number: 94-30988

Library of Congress Cataloging-in-Publication Data
Brown, Joe B., 1948–
Battle fatigue / by Joe B. Brown.
p. cm.
ISBN 0-8054-6154-X
1. Christian life. 2. Stress—Religious aspects—Christianity.
I. Title.
BV4501.2.B7666 1995
248.4—dc20
94-30988
CIP

To My Wife
Teresa
She waited on me to come home from war.
She followed me to seminary and to churches on far-flung fields.
She bore our children
and
helped me conceive and birth this book.
To her and for her I will ever be grateful.

CONTENTS

Introduction: Facing Our Struggles 1

Part 1: Walking when Wounded 5
1. Walking the Distance 7
2. Running the Marathon 25
3. Flying on Eagle's Wings 49

Part 2: Winning the Daily Battles 69
4. Developing Personal Priorities 71
5. Building a Magnificent Marriage 89
6. Prospering in a Profession 111
7. Firming Up Relationships—Through Forgiveness . . 131
8. Surviving when Your Brook Dries Up 153

Part 3: Gaining the Ultimate Victory 173
9. Rebuilding Broken Altars 175
10. Realizing It Is Never Too Late 197

Conclusion: Remembering the Best 219
Endnotes 223

INTRODUCTION

Facing Our Struggles

She came to me on a Sunday morning and the look in her eyes haunted me. It was that hollow look that one expects to see in the eyes of those who have been in combat too long. Her eyes told me that she had fought too many battles and was exhausted by the continuous conflict. "Could God really be concerned with the mundane?" she asked. "Does He care that I'm working nine to five, changing diapers, cooking meals, washing clothes, and struggling to live? There are no great battles being fought in my life, only many little ones."

Then she broke down in tears. "Pastor, I feel so selfish bothering God with my petty complaints. I don't have a life-threatening disease, my kids aren't in trouble, and my family is intact; but so much is going on in my life that I feel overwhelmed by it all. Sometimes I feel like I'm coming apart at the seams. I need a miracle just to keep up the pace. As a Christian, do I have the right to ask God to give me one?"

This woman's experience is not unusual. Unfortunately, according to statistics, 89 percent of Americans suffer from chronic stress syndrome—the kind of stress produced by everyday living. *Battle Fatigue* addresses those life situations that cause Christians to become spiritually, mentally, and emotionally fatigued. This book offers biblical solutions for coping with the tiresome routine. In fact, God is an excellent diagnostician, and no problem is so small that it does not demand His attention.

He knows how we feel. He has successfully treated others who have experienced the same symptoms. We can take heart! Our condition need not be life-threatening; there is a solution for our dilemma. Of course, the solution does not automatically eliminate stress from our lives; rather it is designed to access supernatural power to help overcome the obstacles of life, whether big or small. That power is remarkably available to the average Christian . . . people just like us.

As the pastor of a large church situated in the middle of urban America, I hear the cry of countless people who suffer from battle fatigue. They want to do better, but life's demands always threaten to swamp their little boats. That's because life is full of overloaded boats and unexpected storms. Our options seem limited because most of us cannot walk on water and the shore is out of sight. Our energy is so depleted from the frantic rowing that even swimming and the prospect of keeping our heads above water is out of the question.

Our only hope for rescue comes from the divine lifeguard. That lifeguard is Jesus; the living, resurrected Son of God. He has boundless energy and numerous resources available through a relationship punctuated by fellowship with Him. He has promised to enter our lives and make the living abundant, not just for the "Sweet By and By," but in the nasty, storm-tossed "Now and Now."

Have I just described your feelings? Could you, or someone you know, be suffering from chronic fatigue syndrome? Are your days too long and your nights too short? Do you have too much to do and not enough time to do it? And to make matters worse, are you beginning to think there's no rest in your hectic, seven-day-a-week, twenty-four-hour-a-day schedule? Then read on—I have some good news for you.

In this book you will meet historical figures as well as contemporary Christians who, just like you, struggled daily to stay on course and be what God wanted them to be. They have discovered the biblical principles for persevering. They have determined, by the grace of God, to make the journey called "life," with finishing the course as their goal.

It is time you did the same. Prepare yourself! You are going to fly on the wings of eagles, run with the great men and women of faith, and walk the foreboding valley of the shadows . . . triumphantly maneuvering through life's dangerous mine fields by accessing the power of the living God.

Walking when Wounded

Yet those who wait for the LORD will gain new strength; they will mount up with wings like eagles, they will run and not get tired, they will walk and not become weary.

Isaiah 40:31

The Israelites of Isaiah's day were in exile. After a number of years, they felt that somehow God had overlooked their predicament and was unconcerned about their future. They knew of God's mighty deeds in the past but had trouble sensing His presence and power in their daily lives.

That is not an uncommon dilemma. For most of us it is fairly easy to believe in the infinite power of God, but appropriating that power in our lives to meet daily personal requirements somehow eludes us. Just as Israel had to be reminded that God's power was available, so twentieth-century Christians must also be reminded.

Isaiah's countrymen needed fresh assurance of who God was because He had been replaced in their lives by wooden and metal idols. No wonder the exiled nation was tired and weary and frustrated. Yet God assured them if they would turn back to Him and wait for His promises to be fulfilled in their lives, He would exchange His inexhaustible strength for their weakness. They could walk hundreds of miles to Jerusalem without becoming weary, even to run on occasion, with the vigor and speed of the mighty eagle. But Israel had turned her back on the Lord and for many years forfeited those wonderful blessings.

In many ways we are just like those Israelites. Twentieth-century American Christians suffer from spiritual battle fatigue because we too have filled our lives with too many idols. We have so replaced God in our daily routines that we have lost sight of Him and thereby forfeited His strength in our lives. We have exhausted our own puny store of strength and have become weary and tired with no power for "living." We do not need a preacher to tell us that the world is a graveyard. But the good news of the gospel is that among all of the graves on this planet, one is empty. That makes all the difference.[1]

Part 1, "Walking when Wounded," helps us discover what inhibits our walking, our running, our flying with God. Then, using the delicate instruments of God such as prayer, Bible study, and fellowship, these chapters present a blueprint to get us back on track and rescue us from spiritual battle fatigue.

ONE

Walking the Distance

To talk with God, no breath is lost—
Talk on!
To walk with God, no strength is lost—
Walk on!
To wait on God, no time is lost—
Wait on![1]

We are the self-confessed, upwardly mobile, workaholic generation. We are the risk takers, the adult baby boomers who face each day with intensity, determined to squeeze every ounce of juice from the fruit called "life." Prestige is our aspiration; success is our goal; affluence is our ambition. We believe that with hard work and extra effort, we can realize our potential. So we join the parade of those who dream of being the best—best parent, best business associate, best athlete, best husband, best wife, best student, best at everything.

And then one day we realize that the parade is tiresome, and we are weary. Walking, which seemed so simple, has become exhausting. We have depleted our strength and extinguished our power.

Headed for a Power Outage

What happens when stress leaves us burned out and fatigued? Like the psalmist, we moan, "I am weary with my sighing" (Ps. 6:6), and, "I am weary with my crying" (Ps. 69:3).

Where do we turn when reality hits? Some people grab a "feel good" pill. Others escape through drugs or alcohol.

However, Scripture tells us God equips His children to deal with the dilemmas of life: "Do you not know? Have you not heard? The Everlasting God, the LORD, the creator of the ends of the earth does not become weary or tired. His understanding is inscrutable. He gives strength to the weary and to him who lacks might He increases power" (Isa. 40:28–29).

Noah found that strength as he labored years building an ark in a world where he found neither acceptance nor respect. Abraham gathered up his tents and spent the better part of his life searching for a promised land he had never seen. David actively waited for God's direction in a shepherd's field where he practiced his skills in seclusion—skills that made it possible for him to stand taller than the Philistine giant, Goliath. Daniel bowed his knees to God three times a day in full view of the pagan Babylonians, and in the private pit of Daniel's despair God slipped in and shut the mouths of hungry lions.

True happiness does not come packaged in a pill, nor does it depend upon our circumstances alone. The picture of inner peace and tranquility is graphically displayed for us by Isaiah, the prophet, when he says, "Those who wait for the LORD will gain new strength; they will mount up with wings like eagles, they will run and not get tired, they will walk and not become weary" (Isa. 40:31).

I'd Rather Fly Than Walk

Flying like an eagle, running like an ultramarathoner, walking and never becoming weary—what a glorious dream. In the

Book of Isaiah, the prophet addressed the weighty issues of life. He confronted folks with too much to do and not enough time or energy to do it, folks overcome with the familiar, everyday routine.

There have been times in my life when I have flown like an eagle and God was able to accomplish things through me that I knew I could not have done on my own. I have been able to get up early and stay up late, day in and day out, run like that marathoner, and never become discouraged or bored or burned out. And during those intervals I have literally seen the great wheels of God's purpose revolve and rotate as He licensed me to run beside Him for short periods—until I became winded and slowed the pace.

It is not the flying or the running, but the walking—that daily walking—that gives me trouble. I once heard a story about a persistent snail who started up the trunk of a huge apple tree one cold February day. Painstakingly, as he inched his way upward, a worm poked its head from a crevice in the trunk and said, "You're wasting your energy. There isn't a single apple up there." Undaunted, he continued his laborious climb. "There will be when I get there," he said.[2] You see, excitement causes us to run, and that great supernatural endowment of God-power is what causes us to fly. But walking takes snail-like, patient persistence.

Sometimes the walking is monotonous, one step in front of another on a level plain. Sometimes the walk winds up the side of a mountain where life is bountiful, the air is fresh, and our steps fall light and easy on a grassy path. Then occasionally the trail leads into a dark, putrid valley. There we find ourselves trudging laboriously through swamps of pain and despair.

A good friend of mine, the vice-president of an oil company, was a deacon, faithful Bible study teacher, husband, the father of two little girls; and his passion was flying. In his professional travels he flew a helicopter from one appointment to another, dodging traffic, beating the clock, flying above the crowd. It was quick, easy, and convenient transportation as he effortlessly seesawed from one mountain town to another there in eastern Kentucky.

His love for the sky, his expertise, and his familiarity with the route made it impossible for me to accept what the voice on the other end of the telephone said. "Dead! High voltage wires! Explosion!" I repeated the phrases over and over again in my mind . . . then out loud. Still, I couldn't make myself believe it.

I traveled back to the mountains for the funeral. I saw the hollow look in the eyes of his young wife, the blank stares on two little girls' faces. An obituary notice made a feeble attempt to summarize thirty-four years of a man's life.

I wasn't supposed to be there preaching his funeral—not my young friend. He should have been the one to attend mine, be *my* pallbearer, comfort *my* family. Yet, there I was standing before a woman widowed far too early, children who just wanted their daddy home that night, and friends who had those unspoken questions that always begin with "Why . . . ?"

How are you going to walk when you are wounded? How are you going to move forward when you are fatigued? When you have overslept, and the lunch is not packed, the school bus is honking, and one sneaker is still missing—how can you keep from screaming, "I give up"? When the irritating interruptions of life slap you squarely in the face, how are you going to function effectively and with a genuine smile? When unconfessed sin haunts the hidden corners of your mind, how are you going to get up each morning, whisper a prayer for strength, and handle the self-recrimination—"Haven't you tried this before, and didn't you blow it? What's the use? Why keep struggling?"

How do you maintain your optimism? When your spouse walks out and leaves you with a stack of bills and an empty bank account, how are you going to keep from becoming bitter? When your energy is depleted and your days are too long and your nights are too short, how do you acknowledge the miracles of God and the exhilaration of life—and continue to walk even though you are wounded?

Getting Away from It All

To be honest, sometimes I get tired of walking. Sometimes I want to go to the beach and get away from it all. I want to forget about making beds and mowing lawns and payrolls and promotions and the nine-to-five tedium of life. Sometimes I just want to walk out in the middle of the ocean and allow all the paraphernalia of my life to wash off and out to sea like the rest of the debris on shore. But I have noticed that even when I get to the beach, there are matters like children to feed, laundry to wash, gasoline to pump, and sunburn.

You see, as much as we would like to, we can't go to the beach or the mountains or the desert or anywhere else and escape life. It's there waiting for us. I grew up in the mountains and the folk I knew there are much like the folk anywhere else. I also lived in a beach resort area, and I discovered that the people who live there carry on with life just as everyone else does.

If we lack the ability to carry on in Charlotte or Birmingham or New York City, then we can expect exhaustion to wait for us in the mountains. If we are not walking in the strength of God on a daily basis in Arizona or Texas or Michigan, we will not experience His power in a resort area. The power for walking does not flow out of human strength, but godlike persistence.

When Isaiah used the word "walk," he had more in mind than "walking to the back door," or "walking into the kitchen," or "walking to the refrigerator." The Hebrew word means "setting out on a journey with a goal in mind." Though not a journey specifically earmarked "joy" or a vacation journey, it is indeed the journey of "life."

It was the same kind of journey the children of Israel faced. They were living in Babylon as prisoners of war, refugees who were thousands of miles away from their homeland. In response to their prayers, God began to open the door for them to go back. He gave them a choice: "You can choose freedom rather than slavery. You can go home. I have heard your prayers. Now, at your very fingertips, at the doorstep of your lives, is the opportunity to walk."

However, between the Israelites and their homeland were endless miles of desert, wastelands, mountains, valleys, and wild animals. It would be an unnerving, unending, unyielding journey. They had no airplanes, automobiles, or buses. The only way to get home was to walk. And for many of them, walking seemed out of the question because they suffered from the POW syndrome.

Prisoners of Weakness

POWs, "Prisoners of Weakness," have great difficulty walking, especially when it requires faith. Instead of taking God at His word and relying on His goodness, constancy, and provision, POWs base their walk on current events, the latest fashion trends, the shape of the stock market. Because of this, they sometimes develop a spiritual paralysis that exhibits itself in both physical and behavioral symptoms. Listed below are some symptoms of POW syndrome:

- Indigestion, upset stomach, and ulcers
- Shortness of breath and chest pains
- Headaches, muscle pain, fatigue, boredom
- Temper tantrums, irritability, and mood swings
- Forgetfulness, inability to concentrate, and insomnia

Consider this simple test to see whether or not you are experiencing one or more symptoms of POW syndrome. Place a check beside the statements that pertain to you.

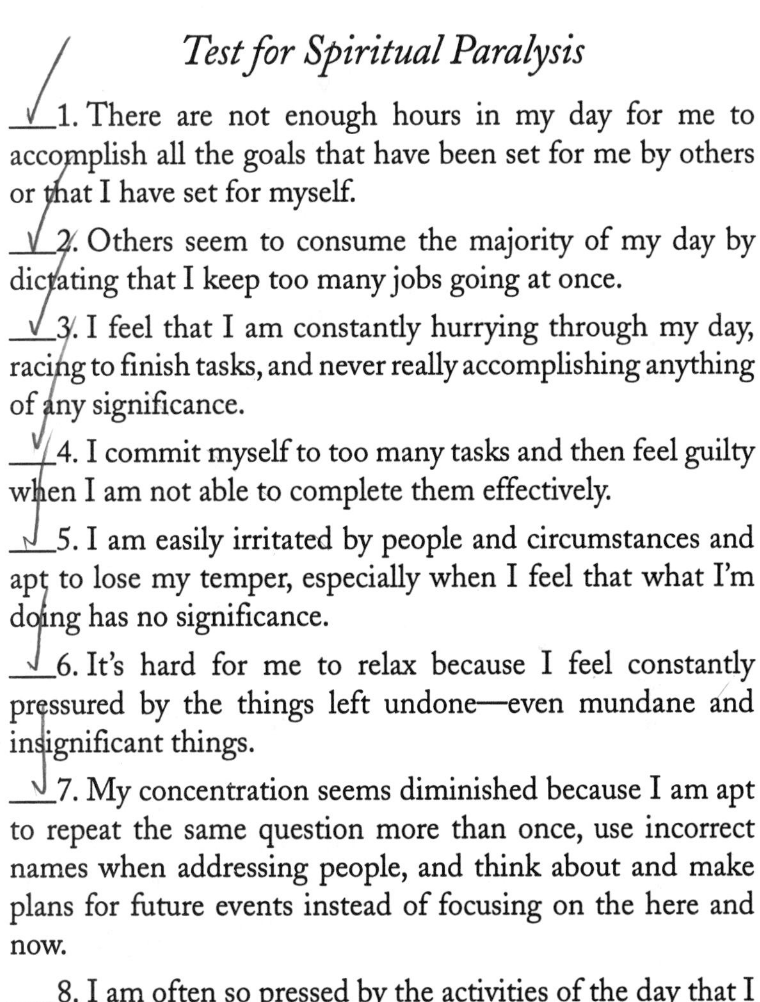

Test for Spiritual Paralysis

___1. There are not enough hours in my day for me to accomplish all the goals that have been set for me by others or that I have set for myself.

___2. Others seem to consume the majority of my day by dictating that I keep too many jobs going at once.

___3. I feel that I am constantly hurrying through my day, racing to finish tasks, and never really accomplishing anything of any significance.

___4. I commit myself to too many tasks and then feel guilty when I am not able to complete them effectively.

___5. I am easily irritated by people and circumstances and apt to lose my temper, especially when I feel that what I'm doing has no significance.

___6. It's hard for me to relax because I feel constantly pressured by the things left undone—even mundane and insignificant things.

___7. My concentration seems diminished because I am apt to repeat the same question more than once, use incorrect names when addressing people, and think about and make plans for future events instead of focusing on the here and now.

___8. I am often so pressed by the activities of the day that I have very little or no time for Bible reading, prayer, or devotions. I'm just too tired.

___9. Church and its related activities only add weight to the pressures of my life so I don't attend regularly; or if I do attend, it's sometimes out of habit or just to relieve me of the guilt that accompanies nonattendance.

__10. Even though I desire it and know it's necessary, I have not appropriated time to develop a personal relationship and intimate fellowship with God. Therefore, it's easy for sin to creep into my life and riddle me with constant guilt for not being able to do better.

How did you score? If you checked one to three blanks, you are in fairly good shape. Four to six indicates definite signs of POW syndrome. And if you scored above six, you have a full-blown case of spiritual paralysis.

Deciding to Walk Is the First Step

Sometimes it is easier to stay in prisons of our own making than to break the chains of bondage. Sometimes it is easier to go to bed and lie on that hard mattress of bitterness than to get up and walk. Freedom brings with it a new and frightening set of responsibilities. What about the Israelites who had the choice of leaving Babylon and captivity? Knowing the rigors of the trip, only fifty thousand of them decided to walk. Two hundred and fifty thousand remained behind.

During the Vietnam War a Mobile Army Surgical Hospital (M.A.S.H.) unit prepared for the onslaught of helicopters with their cargo of dead and dying. They used a system of triage to categorize the victims by the severity of their wounds. One color tag was placed on the dying, those who could not be saved by the inadequate makeshift M.A.S.H. facilities. These were the ones tagged hopeless. A second color tag was attached to those whose wounds were superficial. Their tags indicated that they needed medical attention, yet they would heal. The last color was placed on the bodies of those young men who were in critical condition, but with extra effort from the medical staff, they might survive. They were tagged possibly salvageable.

Into this dismal environment a critically injured boy was carried. With a quick, cursory examination the decision was made that nothing could be done to prevent his death, so a painkiller was administered, and he was tagged hopeless and left to die. Since he was still conscious, a kind nurse decided to stand beside his bed to comfort him, and in talking with the boy she discovered that he was from her hometown back in America. As he lovingly spoke of the home and family that he would never again see, her heart went out to him in his pain. Without explanation, she reached down, removed the tag marked hopeless, and replaced it with one that read salvageable. Because of that act of kindness, he lives today.

Some of us want a winning walk, but we are afraid to take that first step. Perhaps long ago someone made a mistake and placed the wrong tag on us, one that says goof-off, stupid, accident, or loser. And we have believed that label for years. Like children, most of us stand looking up, waiting to hear when to go to bed, when to get up, what to do with our time, what to do with our talents, how to make our decisions. God, however, comes to us and whispers, "I'm here to change the tag. I have not made you to be the slave of whims and fancies or other peoples' opinions. I have made you to walk victoriously with Me, to talk with Me, to have complete fellowship with Me, to make this journey called life with Me. Only under these circumstances, with your hand securely in Mine, can you walk and not become weary."

Spiritual Dehydration Drains Energy

"Weary" is another interesting word. The King James Version of the Bible literally says "faint." The Hebrew word implies that weariness is a feeble condition brought on by old age. And the idea of not growing weary, in spite of the processes of life, implies that God will make us confident and agile even when we no longer appear to be sure-footed. This is not natural, man-made strength; it is supernatural strength.

Are you ready to collapse from exhaustion in the desert of your life? Then the diagnosis is clear: You're suffering from spiritual dehydration. Without God to point us in the direction of the hidden fresh-water springs, our dry carcasses will become prey to all the evils that stalk the deserts of our lives.

Our energy, which once seemed sufficient, has waned because during our trek additional burdens have been placed on our backs. We notice that we are even responsible for carrying other people, an obligation we did not have yesterday. The weariness is always there. There is a dread in our hearts, a nagging fear in our souls.

She was behind the counter in a fast-food restaurant. When I looked past her bifocals and graying hair I could tell she was a woman in her mid-fifties. I knew the answer even before I asked the question, "How are you today?"

"Tired," she whispered. "I don't mean to complain. I know there are a lot of folks worse off than me, but I'm so tired."

"Did you get up early to come into work this morning?" I asked.

"Mister," she replied, "It seems like I've been working all my life."

Such are the realities of life. We all grow weary. According to Isaiah 40:30, even "youths grow weary and tired, and vigorous young men [those with unlimited energy] stumble badly." Sometimes we all lose our grip. Sometimes we all drop our appointed load. Sometimes we all need assistance in getting back up on our feet.

Waiting Is the Key

We cannot escape life, but we can overcome the obstacles of life. Isaiah said, "Though youths grow weary and tired, and vigorous young men stumble badly, yet, those who wait for the LORD . . . will walk and not become weary" (Isa. 40:30–31). Notice, this is not contingent upon being young or being intelligent or being from a good family or having a good education or being wealthy. It is, however, contingent upon one thing: waiting on the Lord. Waiting on the Lord is the key to walking and not becoming weary.

It encourages me to know that Jesus also confronted weariness and exhaustion. There were constant demands on His time and energy. There was always someone to heal or someone to teach. There was always something to explain to the disciples. There were always the challenges—the continual, exasperating threats of the Pharisees, who were on the lookout for a way to trap Him.

When the burdens of life were pressed on Him, Jesus prayed. As He prayed to the Father, He was reinvigorated, quickened, instantly exuberant. He looked at the hollow, empty eyes of that ragtag group of disciples and then He held out His arms and proclaimed with the voice of God, "Come to Me, all who are weary and heavy-laden, and I will give you rest. Take my yoke upon you, and learn from Me, for I am gentle and humble in heart; and you shall find rest for your souls. For My yoke is easy, and My load is light" (Matt. 11:28–30). Then the kind and gentle Savior led those hungry men into a grain field and allowed them to replenish their bodies with food as they picked the heads of grain and ate.

What Jesus said to the disciples also applies to us.This is a lesson on living in His strength and power, not our own. God has placed us in this life and He alone can enable us to walk through life victoriously. His desire is that our Christianity, our faith in Him, be so viable that in it we will walk and not become weary. He wants us to be like Him—linked to the power source—God.

Now if we are to be like Jesus, we must act and react as Jesus does. We must learn from Jesus. What had Jesus just experienced? He had been wearied by the road, causing both His body and His spirit to become famished. What did He do? Did He look for the nearest burger stand so He and His disciples could grab a double cheeseburger and fries? No, His first priority was spiritual food. The Bible says He began to pray to His Father, and as He prayed, that supernatural vigor flowed through Him and to His weary followers.

The same equation works for us: prayer to God + fellowship with God = spiritual renewal from God. Or to put it in other words, with daily prayer and fellowship, God will put "pep in your step" and a "glide in your stride."

Just as God spoke to the children of Israel long ago, He speaks to us. His admonition is:

> You can stay in bondage in Babylon, but your walking will be laborious. Or you can choose to journey with Me, and even though we walk through the dry, barren desert, you'll not grow weary, you will have strength for the trip. I'll give you supernatural strength to carry your load across the expanse of time and climb the mountains of fear, dread, and tedium. Yes, I may lead you to places that you would not have chosen. I'll take you down roads that, given a choice, you might have avoided. But the journey is easier if you walk hand in hand with Me than if you stay in the so-called safely and security of your self-made Babylon.

It Is So Hard to Wait

Are you interested in the power that will invigorate you for the journey?

Are you wondering, "How can I get this? How can the refreshing power be applied to my life? How much does this cost? What do I have to do?"

Well, first of all, it cannot be bought. Second, it is not something that's based on performance. Read the Scripture once again: "Yet those who wait for the LORD . . . , They will walk and not become weary" (Isa. 40:31). Take note of that word *wait.* Waiting is almost un-American. We do not like to wait. We expect instant breakfast, instant service, instant attention. And sometimes we get the impression that we have a remote-control God. Just push the right button, say the right words, and there He is, ready to serve us—instantly.

It just does not work that way. No matter what we have read in books, learned in conferences, or seen on television, we cannot put God in a little wish box and bribe Him, by hook or crook, to be our own personal Santa Claus. No, the God we serve is more interested in us than in our want lists—even if what we want seems "spiritual." Waiting goes against our nature. Why does God require us to wait on Him? Let me explain this way.

Once I remember my daddy taking me to a parade when I was a little boy. We traveled to a neighboring city, Bristol, Virginia, to watch the annual band festival. Over sixty bands were to march that day. I was so excited. He drove his pickup truck and I knew it was going to be a great day.

After we found a parking space, my dad scouted around to find a place for me to sit so that I would not miss a thing when the action started. As I settled in on the edge of that concrete sidewalk, I began to look around. I saw people scattered along the sidewalk, waiting just as I was. I saw an empty street, but to my dismay, I did not see anything that even resembled a parade.

My dad had told me that the parade was scheduled to start at nine o'clock that morning. It was already nine thirty, and I still did not see a parade. People kept saying, "Just be patient, in about fifteen minutes . . . ." When you are five years old, fifteen minutes is an eternity. Soon, though, off in the distance, I could hear a drum, and I knew something was happening . . . somewhere. Yet, even though I strained my eyes, I still did not see a parade.

Moments later, I saw the crowd beginning to stir and then cheer; and I heard a band playing. It was not long before I saw the twirling majorette and the high-stepping drum major, and with wide eyes I watched as the long-awaited parade passed before me.

Wait a minute! Had I not been told that the parade was to start at nine o'clock? But it was almost ten o'clock before I saw the first band. What happened? "Son," my father explained, "the parade started right on time, at nine, just as you were told. But it took the parade an hour to get to where you were." Before I could experience the sights and hear the sounds, I had to wait for the parade to get to me.

The parade has already started. Oh, it might not be in front of you yet. You might not be able to see the festivities at this point, but if you are ever to see it—if you are ever to experience God and His parade of power and strength and victory in your life—you have to get on the route, adjust your clock to God's time schedule, watch, listen, and wait. Wait . . . in anxious anticipation.

Keys to Waiting

Waiting does not always mean sitting by idly. There are things we can do, disciplines we can learn, and priorities we can change while we wait.

Worship by Placing God First in Your Life. Each morning, as we rise from our beds, we can acknowledge His existence. We can give thanks for His provisions just as the psalmist who wrote, "When I remember Thee on my bed, I meditate on Thee in the night watches, for Thou hast been my help, and in the shadow of Thy wings I sing for joy" (Ps. 63:6–7). Recommitting ourselves to Him and His plan for our lives each day; recounting His faithfulness in little things: the ability to see, to hear, to speak, to touch; marveling at His capacity for loving; asking Him for a fresh start on a new day, every day—all of these are part of our worship.

Spend Time in His Word. It is reported that a pastor walked into a children's Sunday School class one morning. "Who broke down the wall of Jericho?" quizzed the pastor, testing the kids' Bible knowledge. One small boy, seemingly annoyed by the inquiry, spontaneously replied, "Not me, Sir!"

Visibly shaken, the pastor looked at the equally puzzled teacher and said, "Is this typical?"

"No, pastor," was her apologetic reply. "The boy is a trusted and honest child, and if you want my opinion, I really don't think he did it."

He turned to the Sunday School superintendent and listened in amazement as he heard, "I've known the boy and his family for a long time, and I just can't picture any of them doing such a terrible thing."

With that response the chairman of deacons interrupted the conversation and said, "Pastor, let's not make a big issue of this. Let's just pay for the damages and charge it to our maintenance account."

Do you realize only 45 percent of professing Christians read the Bible on a weekly basis and only 12 percent open the Book daily? Is it any wonder that we are weak and ineffective when it comes to our spiritual walk?

The Bible is not an obsolete document written by outmoded saints. It is addressed to us and is applicable to our lives. We must get to know Him. The best way to do that is to read His letter, the Bible. As a young man aboard a naval vessel, I remember being homesick on more than one occasion. Letters from home were always timely. As I read and reread those letters my relationship with my family was strengthened. I felt close to them and a part of their lives.

That is the way of the Father. He reveals Himself, His love, His promises, His support, His admonitions, His ways,

His plans; and it is all tucked neatly inside His Word. Over and over again in Psalm 119, the psalmist repeats, "I wait for Thy word." And we too must be willing to actively wait, submerged in God's Word. Why? Because it guards us against sin (v. 11), it produces reverence for God (v. 38), it is a trusted counselor (v. 24), a wise teacher (v. 41), it answers our questions (v. 42), and keeps us from being ashamed (v. 46). The Word revives us when we are afflicted (v. 50), shows us the grace of God (v. 58), and His goodness (v. 68). It reveals to us who God is and who we are (v. 73). It makes us wiser, gives us insight, and helps us understand (vv. 98–100). The word is a lamp. In our darkest hour it will keep our feet from stumbling. It is a light to illumine the path God has laid out before us (v. 105). If we are to know God, we must read His Word daily.

Keep Unbroken Communication with God Through Prayer. Prayer unlocks the gates of heaven, and with it we access God. If you feel powerless and anemic in your spiritual walk, check your prayer life. Many Christians are defeated, discouraged, and disheartened simply because they pray so little. Prayer supersedes all laws of the universe because it calls into action the One who is responsible for its creation. This fact alone should stir Christians up to "take hold of God" (Isa. 64:7) and pray.

Yet for many prayer is little more than a frustrating attempt at crisis intervention. Is it any wonder, if we are disconnected from our power source, that we tire so easily under the strain of daily walking? Our lack of prayer is often an accurate measurement for the quality of our service. Little prayer . . . little for God in service. How often do you pray? How much time do you spend in the position of prayer? When the kingdom of heaven can be had for the asking, why don't we pray? The words from an old hymn come to mind.

Oh, what peace we often forfeit!
Oh, what needless pain we bear!
All because we do not carry
Everything to God in prayer.

We can talk to the Lord today . . . and every day. We can share with Him our joy, our pain, our triumphs, our defeats, our burdens, our weariness. By establishing a special time and a special place, we can meet Him, as Daniel did, on a regular daily basis. To walk and not become weary, we must pray.

Fellowship with Other Christians. Fellowship, sometimes translated *koinonia,* has been described as the bond of common purpose and devotion that binds believers together and to Christ. This close association takes place in social, religious, and even business settings. Lone Ranger Christianity can stifle spiritual growth. Encouragement, counsel, and constructive criticism from Christian brothers and sisters are necessary in order to stay on track.

Fellowship involves pumping one another up. I remember swimming in a mountain stream in southwest Virginia, where I grew up. My lifejacket was an old patched inner tube. Ever so often it would start to lose air and I would begin to sink. When that happened, the inner tube had to be pumped full of fresh air. Why? Because it leaked.

Spiritually we leak too. Prayer, Bible study, worship, and fellowship with believers who declare, "You can make it, I'll help you," pump us back up and help to keep us afloat. Your walk encourages others.

The One Who Waits . . . Walks

God promises that if we will patiently but actively wait on Him, we will once more hear a song in our hearts. If we wait upon the Lord, we will smile again and hear the sound of our own laughter. If we wait on the Lord, we will walk and not become weary—and His parade will never pass us by.

We must wait on God—wait until we see Him, until the parade comes to the place where God has planted us. We have to become like a rope, intertwined with God Himself. His personality must become our personality. His life becomes our lives. His motives, His desires, His will—all become ours. And, oh yes, His power becomes our power.

When we wait on God and walk with God, we will not worry about controlling Him; He will control us. We become intertwined with God as He moves into our lives and takes over. When God is in control and directs our lives, life itself becomes an adventure. Life becomes the parade. It becomes an exhilarating experience with God because He is everywhere we go and in everything we do—walking across a desert, getting up and going to work, brushing out the toilet bowl, waiting for a child to finish baseball practice, or playing a game of golf.

This kind of life is not out of reach. It is not something reserved for preachers and teachers and missionaries. No, walking in God's abundant strength is attainable for everyone who is willing to listen and grasp hold of God.

What is that I hear? Listen! Listen closely with your spirit. Is that not a trumpet tuning up? Wait right there—where He has placed you. The parade is on its way.

TWO

Running the Marathon

When things seem difficult, and life uphill,
Don't look too far ahead, keep plodding on,
And inch by inch, the road will shorten, till
The roughest patches will be past and gone,
And you'll look back surprised and cheered to find
That you have left so many miles behind,
And very soon the tedious climb will stop,
And you will stand triumphant at the top.[1]

The runner's face was flushed as he jumped from one boulder to the next in order to stay ahead of the whitecaps crashing against the Scottish coastline. The wind was frigid as it slapped against his unprotected cheek and wrapped his long coat awkwardly around his ankles, making his trek seem clumsy and dangerous.

The runner, however, was oblivious to the risk. Being totally submerged in the exhilaration of the run, he continued to leap over the wet stones until his shiny Wellington boot slipped and missed its landing place, causing his foot to wedge in a narrow crevice and his head to bash against the hard rocks below him.

He lay there, unconscious, for an undetermined period of time. When he awakened, both rain and darkness were falling. Realizing there was little hope for rescue under such conditions, he began the excruciating process of extracting his useless leg from its rocky vise. Only by squatting on his coat, positioning his arms behind him, and flexing the good leg, was he able to thrust himself backwards a few inches at a time up over the rocks and toward the meadow. Many times during that journey back to the guest house where he was staying, he called out to God for help.

Soaked, shivering, and in agonizing pain, he inched his way across the meadow, drifting in and out of consciousness. Through it all he recalls an inaudible voice bombarding his brain with, "Don't give up, Lloyd. Don't give up." He thought of a Bible verse memorized years earlier: "'For I know the plans I have for you,' declares the LORD, 'plans to prosper you and not to harm you, plans to give you hope and a future'" (Jer. 29:11, NIV).

Little did Lloyd Ogilvie know that in the hour of his greatest need, God had already sent a Christian physician on an excursion through that meadow, taking a route that would lead him down the exact path where Lloyd was helplessly lying. Soon the nationally renowned preacher and senior pastor of First Presbyterian Church in Hollywood, California, was medicated and transported from that hostile environment to one of security, warmth, and safety.

"I had run in the fast lane at top speed for years," he wrote later. "Even study times . . . were round-the-clock work periods. And brief vacations were simply to catch my breath so I could start running again. Now I couldn't even walk!"

Even as he was placed in the ambulance after his narrow escape from death, he admitted asking those attending him, "Can't you fix my leg here, give me some crutches, and send me on my way?"[2]

Running Is Hard Work

In running, both feet leave the ground for an instant during each individual stride. Running involves risk, because when walking accelerates into running, we are airborne for a time, knowing that when our feet finally touch ground, it will be far from our last point of contact, quickly placing us in unfamiliar territory.

Running takes strength, vitality, endurance, and energy—definitely more energy than walking. To run is to push at a faster pace, to cover expanded territory, to see less and experience more. When we run, we perspire—not just a little, but a lot. We pant for breath. Our lungs feel as if they will explode. Our mouths are dry. Our muscles ache. Our heart throbs.

Running takes determination, perseverance, and conviction. Whether we are running away from some dread enemy or toward a coveted goal, the experience demands all our concentration. It is a decisive act precipitated by a firm resolution. It is not an exercise for the weak or faint of heart. It is often grueling, demanding, and exhausting.

Strength for the Running

Isaiah 40:31 adds a spiritual dimension to running. "Yet those who wait for [place their hope in] the LORD will gain new strength . . . they will run and not get tired." Like Isaiah, the writer of Hebrews 12:1 encouraged newly converted Jewish believers to "run with endurance the race . . . ." For them the course had been laid out in heaven, the participants' names had been entered on the roster, but the race itself had not yet been run. The Hebrew Christians had professed the faith, but they had not made any attempt to leave the starting line. Perhaps the length of the course, the steep grade, or the diversions along the way had caused them to become distracted and fearful.

During my stint in the Navy I had several occasions to cross the Atlantic Ocean. On one particular crossing, the sea became extremely rough and choppy because of a hurricane in the area. The small naval destroyer was tossed about like a child's toy while that storm played itself out. Several men slept in their lifejackets; some even advocated turning the ship around and aborting the mission.

Then I stood on the bridge with the captain. In the midst of the turmoil, he was calm. His voice never faltered. His face never flinched. His gaze was set firmly on the instrument panel that gave us direction through the blinding storm. As I watched my captain's face and sensed his resolve that we would make it, my anxieties started to slip away and I found in him the strength to weather the storm. That is how we run the race without becoming tired. We find the strength to live the Christian life in our Captain, Jesus Christ.

That is what the disciples did. It had been a long day by the Sea of Galilee. A multitude of people pressed in so tightly to hear His teaching that Jesus was obliged to move His pulpit into one of the boats. When evening came, He was tired and retreated to the stern of the boat to rest while the disciples maneuvered it into the current and headed for the other side of the lake.

During their journey a sudden and violent storm swept across that deep, foreboding basin. The winds were gale force. The waves were breaking over the vessel with such intensity that it was beginning to take on water. Panic inundated the dazed disciples when they realized their energy was spent and their ship was sinking.

As a last resort, the bucket brigade summoned Jesus from His resting place. As He made His way to His frightened disciples, His voice never faltered. His face never flinched. His hands were steady and strong. He did not grab a bucket, nor did He adjust the rudder or hoist the sails. He simply rebuked the wind and spoke to the sea as a mother would quieten an unruly child, saying, "Hush, be still." And at the sound of His voice the wind became a gentle breeze and the sea stopped thrashing about and settled down, perfectly calm. Suddenly those disciples realized that Jesus was the Captain, not just of their vessel, but of their lives. They had run themselves into a state of exhaustion trying to stay afloat and on course—when all they needed was a word from the Captain.

And that is the same thing Lloyd Ogilvie needed. After long months of recuperation, someone asked him how he was going to spend the rest of his life. His response came quickly. His plan was to listen to the Captain's voice, draw on His limitless resources, "and run with Him on two strong legs."[3]

You too may feel shipwrecked by the storms of life, crippled on the treacherous path you have chosen, too tired and weak to continue running. "Hush, be still," and listen for the voice of the Captain. He alone can calm your storm. Only in Him you will find strength to run.

Excuses for Not Running

There are a lot of seemingly legitimate excuses for not running. Our lives are scheduled to the absolute limit. When running is crowded into our already tight schedule, stress develops.

Stress is a serious condition; 75 to 90 percent of all visits made to primary care physicians last year were stress- related disorders and illnesses. Ten years ago most people who frequented health spas went there initially for weight reduction. But today an ever-increasing number of Americans go to clinics for stress reduction. Surrounded by stereo speakers venting soothing New Age music, they slip into their subconscious, get in touch with their karma, simply to discover a deeper level of stress.

Physicians report that 89 percent of us suffer from chronic stress disorder. While human beings were designed for periods of short-term stress, our bodies were never intended to hold up under the effects of chronic stress. When our forefathers ran through the woods and encountered a bear, they experienced short-term stress—because they either ran from the bear, climbed a tree, shot the bear, or were eaten by the bear. In any case, stress was alleviated.

We no longer have time to run through the woods. We walk through crowded concrete canyons in smog-soaked cities. The bear has been replaced by a dysfunctional boss, an unsympathetic corporation that cares more about bottom-line financial statements than people, and by a system that gives little thought to spiritual running.

We are spiritually out of shape. Our doctrinal muscles are flabby, and we feed our minds a mystical junk food diet. We have lost our desire for the fresh air of God that invigorates our bodies as we fill our souls with His presence and run beside Him. Our legs are too weak to support the weight of life. Our energy is depleted.

Recently I found myself along the side of the road with my car sputtering. I knew the tank was empty because the fuel gauge registered E, the warning light was flashing, and the car no longer had the power to move.

I had several options. I could give the car a motivational pep talk. I could make an emotional plea and hope the car would respond by moving onto the highway and toward my destination. I could give the car a hard push into traffic, hoping the oncoming cars would be incentive enough for it to move. I thought about towing it into another neighborhood, giving it a change of scenery, a new paint job, and an oil change to improve its self-image. But realistically I knew that if I did not put some gasoline in that vehicle, it would never run again.

You have probably tried everything too. You have propped yourself up, psyched yourself up, pulled yourself up, fixed yourself up, but you still make excuses for not running with

God. You are tired. You have been running the wrong race, for the wrong reason, with the wrong motives; your race will take you to the point of exhaustion, but will never take you to God (see Gal. 2:2).

We live in a nation that knows the price of everything but the value of nothing. We are becoming like Esau, who was more interested in his appetite than his birthright. We are like Lot, who followed the path of least resistance, going where the grass looked greenest and the business opportunities seemed ripest. We are the prodigal son, demanding our fair share and somehow erroneously convinced that a small nest egg will be a hedge against all the hardships of life.

It Is Possible to Run in the Wrong Direction

It is possible to run away from God as the story of Elijah demonstrates. Even though he was used mightily by God, we easily identify with Elijah because he "was a man with a nature like ours" (Jas. 5:17). He had physical, emotional, and spiritual ups and downs. He experienced stress and fatigue, as we do.

Elijah had stood on Mount Carmel and watched breathlessly as God's all-consuming presence rushed from the portals of heaven and etched His signature in fire on the face of that mountain. The encounter ended as quickly as it began; the onlookers left, the sky darkened, the rains came, and Elijah was left alone with a death threat from Jezebel, the queen. With his energy spent, his body tired, his mind troubled, he "was afraid and arose and ran for his life" (1 Kings 19:3).

Elijah did what many of us do when we feel alone and threatened. He ran. He thought if he could put as much distance as possible between himself and Jezebel, he would find peace and safety. Yet, instead of freeing him, his running only added to his exhaustion because he was trying to run in his own diminished energy. He was not running with God; he was not running to God.

Finally, he came to the end of his own strength, fell in a pitiful heap at the base of a juniper tree, and slept. As he slept, an angel hovered over him, making a fire, preparing a cake of bread, filling a jar with water. Twice Elijah was instructed to "Arise, eat, because the journey is too great for you" (1 Kings 19:7). Twice he filled his stomach with heavenly food and drink. The Bible says, "He went in the strength of that food forty days and forty nights" (1 Kings 19:8).

Sometimes we, like Elijah, try to run on sheer emotional energy. That energy may be fueled by fear, anger, hatred, or even love. That kind of energy will not take us far, and sometimes it may even take us in the wrong direction. Any journey we attempt in our own strength will end in exhaustion, disappointment, and frustration. But with a daily portion of heavenly food our energy will be replenished and we will find the strength for prolonged running. As Jesus said, "I am the bread of life; he who comes to Me shall not hunger, and he who believes in Me shall never thirst" (John 6:35).

Are You a Spiritual Hitchhiker?

The hitchhiker wants a free ride. He assumes no responsibility for the money needed to purchase the car, the fuel to run it, or the cost of upkeep. He anticipates a comfortable ride, plus safety. He presumes on the driver's insurance to cover him in case of a mishap. He may even ask the driver to take him to a specific location, even though it may involve extra miles or inconvenience.

This world is full of spiritual hitchhikers. They seem to have settled the question concerning salvation, and they may even attend church. They want all the benefits and privileges associated with being a Christian, but none of the responsibilities. A spiritual hitchhiker has no accountability. He wants convenience without commitment. His desire is to be served rather than to serve.

I have known of several people who could be classified as spiritual hitchhikers. The one I remember most clearly was a country music star. He married a beautiful young woman and rose to national stardom all in the same year. People flocked to hear him sing in the popular southern night club where he was employed.

But a day came when he realized the emptiness of his lifestyle. He knew there had to be more to living than what dark night clubs had to offer. So he gave his life, his music, and his home to Jesus Christ.

Now he realized that the atmosphere where he worked made him very uncomfortable. Wanting to make a clean sweep and break free from his past, he confided in the night club operator his intentions to quit. But his uncaring boss reminded him, "Remember, I own your contract. If you leave me, you'll never make another dime in the music business as long as you live."

"I own your contract—I own you!" That's what the country music star heard, and when he balanced a lucrative bank account against the eternal benefits of serving Jesus Christ, the jingle of the coins drowned out the gentle voice of the Savior. He was a spiritual hitchhiker, parading his experience, carried by emotionalism—but he never learned to run.

How about you? Who is calling the shots in your life? Who or what owns your contract? Which earthly sound captivates your attention? According to Jesus, it is impossible to serve the god of this world plus Jehovah God. "For either [you] will hate the one, and love the other, or else [you] will hold to one, and despise the other. You cannot serve God and mammon" (Luke 16:13). Are you a spiritual hitchhiker, trying to hold onto God with one hand and the things of this world with the other? If so, let go! You will discover new aspirations and challenges only when you decide to give up hitchhiking to run with God.

Running Demands Commitment

Running with God is exhilarating, but it is never effortless. As a high school track participant, I ran the mile. Most of the race was a blur. The finish line was out of sight, and the starting line was a distant memory. All I could hear while running were people's voices and the steady beat of my feet on the track. I remember the sensation of gasping for air when it seemed I couldn't get enough oxygen. My heart raced. My legs felt numb. At some point in every race I came to my threshold of pain where my mind said, "You fool! Quit! Stop the race!"

That's what happened to the young ruler who stood before Jesus in Luke 18. He was well dressed, well educated, and seemingly well prepared for life. Only one nagging question kept him awake during the night, so there he was, asking Jesus, "What shall I do to inherit eternal life?" (Luke 18:18).

"Run the race," Jesus said, "You know the commandments. Keep them."

"Sir, I have done all these things since I was just a boy," he proudly reported, assuming eternal life could be had by accumulating enough good deeds and righteous practices.

"There's just one thing you lack, then," replied Jesus. "Do the ultimate good deed. Sell all of your possessions. Give the profits to the poor. Then come and run with Me. I'll give you treasures in heaven."

The crowd watched the expression on his face change. A voice in his head seemed to scream, "You fool! Quit! Stop!" And he turned and walked away, unwilling even to start the race.

Running with the Savior demands total commitment. During His earthly ministry, Jesus had thousands of followers. One day when the multitudes were following close at His heels, watching for another miracle, waiting for another meal, He turned and looked at them and said, "If anyone comes to

Me, and does not hate [by comparison of his love for Me], his own father and mother and wife and children and brothers and sisters, yes, and even his own life, he cannot be My disciple" (Luke 14:26).

"Count the cost," He seemed to say. "It's not an easy run. When you follow Me, you head in the same direction that I am headed . . . toward a cross." There is a cost involved in refusing: "Whoever does not carry his own cross and come after Me cannot be My disciple" (Luke 14:27).

You Choose Your Own Race

Christmas in Paducah, Kentucky, had been wonderful that year. Some snow had fallen, but the old home place was cozy and warm. A roaring fire in the family room, holiday smells coming from the kitchen, the tinseled cedar tree, talk of the old days, and all that laughter made it seem like the front of a nostalgic Christmas card. The grandparents had immediately fallen in love with the new baby. She was the first grandchild and she was beautiful. Her young parents were so proud. Her daddy had made that long trip from his pastorate in Alabama just to show her off to his folks.

The weather was clear but very cold that morning they headed back to Alabama. The baby fell asleep almost immediately, so the young pastor persuaded his wife to drive while he grabbed a few minutes of study time for Sunday's sermon.

South of Paducah and north of Nashville, their journey took them across a long bridge where the moisture in the air had condensed, forming a thin layer of ice and a dense fog. As their van crossed the bridge, it hit a patch of that ice, the pastor's wife lost control, and they slammed tightly against the guardrail. Thankfully, no one was hurt, but the van had made a 180-degree turn and was headed in the wrong direction on that foggy bridge.

Sensing the possible danger, the pastor knew he had to get his family out of the van and to the other side of the road while he attempted to turn the vehicle in the right direction. But no sooner had his wife stepped out on the asphalt with the baby in her arms than a car came out of the fog, sliding toward them, also out of control. When the car struck the van, it pinned her against the guardrail, and the force of the blow knocked the baby out of her arms and over the railing.

Instantly the pastor was standing beside his frantic wife. The fog was so thick they could hardly see one another, let alone determine the fate of their only child. Without hesitation that daddy made a decision, climbed to the place where he had last seen his baby, and jumped—over the railing, into the impenetrable fog, all for the sake of love.

He could not have known that in an attempt to rescue his child, he was plunging to his death on the rocky embankment below. There was no water in that part of the lake.

The choices we make do matter. Sometimes, in a split second, life strikes a blow, and we are forced to make choices that affect our lives and the lives of those around us. Sometimes those choices are not based on rationality or the facts, but on emotions such as fear, anger, panic, jealousy, or even love.

Running always involves choices. We can choose the terrain on which we run, the altitude, and sometimes even the climate. We can choose the difficulty of the run, the length of the run, and the time we will spend running. But the most important choice we will make concerning running is the type of race we enter. When we choose the race, we lock ourselves into a predetermined course. We voluntarily give up our rights to determine where we will run, the difficulty of the run, or how much time we will spend running. Our primary responsibility after choosing the race is to finish.

Isaiah insisted that it is possible to run and not become tired. "Yet those who wait for the LORD will gain new strength;

. . . They will run and not get tired" (40:31). The word *tired* literally means running so hard and so long that we gasp for breath and faint for lack of strength. This tiredness is not precipitated by the load we carry, but by the duration of the physical, emotional, mental, and spiritual run. This "tired" is a weariness that tears at our souls and drains our inner being.

It is caused by the treadmill effect of living. No matter how fast we move, no matter how long we run, no matter how much energy we put forth, we just do not seem to be going anywhere. We head our life in one direction, run as hard and fast as we can, and then when we reach that horizon, the only thing we see beyond it is another horizon and another and another. We might as well be on a treadmill because we are really not making any headway. We start to ask ourselves, "Am I going in the right direction? Am I doing the right things? Is life supposed to be like this? I thought it would be easier. After all, I'm a Christian!" We each choose our own race. Some choose the rat race and live with the consequences; others choose the Redeemer's race and reap the rewards.

The Rat Race

Sometimes the road we travel takes on the look of an army's route of retreat. Its perimeters are littered with the bodies of wounded soldiers who have not made it. Gunned down by the enemy and too exhausted to go on, they are paralyzed by worry about what might happen, grief stricken by what has happened, and suffering because of what is happening. They are angered because of their inability to change things, exasperated because they seem to be accomplishing nothing, irritated because their problems will not go away, and vexed and annoyed because they face the same hard run everyday. They are tired to the point of gasping for breath. They have chosen the wrong race.

The rat race is that undefined, man-made sprint, assigned to each of us at birth, with the potential to sap the energy from our very lives. This race has no attainable goals. It is never ending; there is no starting point or finish line. The rat race points us in the direction of the second floor and then positions us on the down escalator. We can never get ahead because all the odds are stacked in the rat's favor. In the rat race, the rat always wins.

Yes, there are temporary rewards. Take Mac, for instance. He participated in the rat race. Employed by a Fortune 500 company, Mac and his wife traveled to Hawaii twice. They even toured Europe. But when he returned to the States, the company always demanded he do more and more and more. One day, completely drained of potential and energy, Mac was told that he had been replaced by a new man, with a younger heart, stronger legs, cheaper hospitalization, and a smaller pay check. Mac moved out of his posh office. He was allowed to stay with the company, but in a lesser position with no hope for promotions, perks, or power . . . all the things deemed important in the rat race. Mac coped by smoking pot and snorting coke. Eventually, he gave up on the rat race and the human race.

The Redeemer's Race

But it doesn't have to be like that. We can choose which race we will run. The Redeemer's race offers excellent rewards for those who run.

God's Rest. First, the Redeemer's race includes "R and R"—rest and relaxation. The writer of Hebrews 4:1 concluded, "Therefore, let us fear lest, while a promise remains of entering His rest, any one of you should seem to come short of it." We can endure the race of life because Christ promises periods of rest during the run. *Rest* comes from a Greek word meaning "down from," and is used with the idea of motion. It is the concept of coming "down from" the state of constant motion. Rest carries with it the notion of coming out of the heat of the run, refitting, and then getting back into the race. It is a voluntary decision by the Christian to cease forward motion and come aside—not to quit, but to momentarily do something else.

The military term for this type of rest is called "standing down." Standing down does not mean that you go off somewhere and simply stare into space. It is not couch-potato inactivity. Standing down is when the captain momentarily pulls his troops aside—out from the battle, away from the war, off the front line—to freshen them.

During the stand down the troops get a hot meal, a warm shower, and a bed that is safe and quiet. They are allowed to collect their thoughts. During this time fresh troops come into the captain's outfit. New recruits bring fresh energy, new enthusiasm, and revived determination to win the battle. Then, after receiving new weapons and updated training, the reinvigorated squad is sent back to the front line to bring home the victory.

God's Power. Second, the Redeemer's race is inspired by, fueled by, chartered by, and charted by God Himself. In contrast, the rat race was contrived by man. "Let us run with endurance the race that is set before us, fixing our eyes on Jesus" (Heb. 12:1–2).

We are to run the race that God has set before us and the goal is not to compete or to keep up with other runners. The goal is to finish the race, and the only way to finish the race is by running with endurance.

Albert was a brilliant man, a physician, an accomplished musician. He knew he was in the rat race, and he sensed burnout in his life. He had received rewards for his accomplishments: worldwide recognition, wealth, accolades from the masses.

Yet he was wise enough to know it would not last. More than once he sat in a dark room, alone, being honest with himself, and thought, *I am empty. I am not fulfilled. This is not the race God has called me to run.*

Some still call Albert Schweitzer a fool for what he did. Leaving his lucrative practice and forsaking his wonderful organ, he went to Lambarene in French Equatorial Africa. There, in a run-down chicken coop, he began to practice medicine. He treated all who came to him. When his makeshift hospital needed more space, he used his Nobel Peace Prize money, all $33,000 of it, to enlarge the facility.

He started a leper colony. And there he found purpose for his life and peace for his soul. He had the potential for power and fame, but he spent his life in an uncharted area and served for no other reason than love. He ran the Redeemer's race.

He is not alone either. People like David Livingstone and Mother Teresa chose a similar race. The apostle Peter left the comfortable surroundings of his home in Galilee and forsook his family and his business to follow a carpenter destined for death on a cross. The apostle Paul, by his own admission, left position, fame, and reputation, all the rewards of the rat race, and counted them as animal refuse in light of what he had received from Jesus Christ. Our Lord Himself left the halls of heaven, the throne of the universe, to be born in an animal shelter, to live in what most would consider a hick town on the nowhere road to nothing, to be crucified for no other reason than love. That is the Redeemer's race.

The rat race or the Redeemer's race? The choice seems obvious. Sometimes, though, it is difficult to sort out the competing claims on our lives. How can we know which race we are choosing?

Making the Choice

During the Depression, many were without work. A young man read a newspaper advertising employment in a telegraph office. Quickly he dressed and found himself in a room filled with others seeking the same job. In his despair, he dismissed thoughts of employment. After all, there were already too many applicants in the room. What chance did he have?

As he was about to leave, he noticed the steady hum of dot, dot, dash in the room. Suddenly he stood, walked into a small inner office, spoke briefly with the clerk, and then came out with the job.

"We demand an explanation," cried the rest of the waiting applicants.

"Oh, it's simple," confessed the young man. "As I sat, waiting my turn for an interview, I began to listen to the sounds in the room. One sound stood out, the dots and dashes coming from the inner office. As I listened more intently, the message in the dots and dashes became clear. 'If you can understand this, come in the office. The job is yours.' I simply listened and obeyed."

Listen to the Right Voices

Does your heart long to have a word from God? Do you desire uninterrupted communion with Him? Are you listening? Here it is. "Those who wait for the Lord will gain new strength; . . . They will run and not get tired" (Isa. 40:31). And where does the strength come from? "In repentance and rest you shall be saved, in quietness and trust is your strength" (Isa. 30:15).

When Isaiah wrote this passage, the idolatrous nation of Israel was insecure and frightened. They found that they could not depend on the weather patterns to produce enough food or provide enough water for their daily needs. There was a constant danger from enemies who threatened to annihilate the small, struggling nation. They were restless, wandering from place to place, seeking nourishment and protection. There was little stability in their lives. They continually worried about the present as well as the future.

Into this chaotic atmosphere Isaiah interjected an interesting hypothesis. His assertion was that security, safety, and provision will come from God only after Israel repented and rested. Repentance meant "a return to God." It meant turning their backs on silly superstitions and powerless idols that had pervaded their once monotheistic culture. Repentance meant pursuing that dynamic living relationship with God that would put them back on the right track, turn their hearts in the right direction, and eventually lead them home.

The word *rest* means "a lying down, an assurance of provision and security." It is confidence that God will provide for every need. This type of rest is pictured in Psalm 23:

"The Lord is my shepherd, I shall not want." He directs my path. I can rest in His leadership.

"He makes me lie down in green pastures; He leads me beside quiet waters." He provides for all my needs. I can rest in His provision.

"He restores my soul; He guides me in the paths of righteousness for His name's sake." He heals me emotionally and spiritually. When I am weak of body and weary of soul, His Word is a "lamp unto my feet, and a light unto my path" (Ps. 119:105). I can rest in His direction for my life.

"Even though I walk through the valley of the shadow of death, I fear no evil; for Thou art with me; Thy rod and Thy staff, they comfort me." When I'm alone and scared, I feel His touch and I'm comforted. I can rest in His presence.

"Thou dost prepare a table before me in the presence of my enemies; Thou hast anointed my head with oil; My cup overflows." Great joy floods my soul as I realize my position in His flock. I can rest in His unmerited favor.

"Surely goodness and lovingkindness will follow me all the days of my life, and I will dwell in the house of the Lord forever."

Because God is good and His lovingkindness abounds toward me, I have a bright future. I can rest in His salvation. Truly, I shall not want.

Trust God to Do His Part

R. H. Macy failed seven times before his department store in New York caught on. English novelist John Creasey got 753 rejection slips before he eventually published 564 books. Babe Ruth struck out 1,330 times, but also hit 714 home runs.

Every soul who has attempted to run has stumbled, fallen, and even lost his way. It takes God-given determination to start the race and God-given strength to complete it. "In quietness and trust is your strength" (Isa. 30:15). That "quietness" implies ceasing all interfering activity in order to take time to recognize the awesome power of God, knowing it is available and accessible. It means being still in order to hear His voice. It is trusting and having confident assurance that God will do His part even when we can't—or won't.

In frustration, Jennifer Johnson banged her hands on the steering wheel of her car. "I can't believe it," she screamed out loud. Earlier that morning she had intended to stop for gas, but she had forgotten. Now it was dark, she was in the wrong section of town, her gas tank was empty, and she was scared.

Through the twilight smog, she could barely make out the silhouettes of large warehouses, railroad tracks, and chain link fences. As she reached to lock her doors, her eyes searched the area for a friendly restaurant, gas station, or telephone booth. But there was nothing. *Maybe sooner or later a police car will drive by,* she thought, and slumped down in the seat to wait.

Then she saw him. Her heart began to pound uncontrollably as the form of a man made his way down the middle of the street, coming straight toward her car. *Maybe he won't see me. Maybe he'll just walk on by,* she closed her eyes and prayed. But when she looked up, he was standing at the window, tapping on the glass.

Instantly she became hysterical. She screamed, "Get away! Leave me alone!" Yet he only intensified his tapping, yelling something, but Jennifer could not hear him over her own screams. Unable to enter her car through the windows, the man tried the doors. Now perspiring heavily, she began blowing the horn, and to her relief he left.

However, in a short time he was back, this time with a steel bar. Shattering the windows, he was able to unlock the door and reached to grab her arm. Sliding away from him in fear, she kicked at his face, crushing his nose. Bleeding, he pulled her, reluctant and crying, from the car. When he loosened his grip on her arm, she scooted away from him and prepared to defend herself. Still dazed from the blow, he stood, trembling, wiping the blood from his battered and bruised face.

That is when she saw the flashing lights approaching in the dark night. A strange rumbling noise increased in volume as the ground began to tremble underneath her feet. She watched the monstrous train roar past, crash into her disabled car, and drag it, totally demolished, down the railroad tracks.[4]

God knows best. Trust Him.

Cultivate the Right Attitude

The rat race is bent on accumulating things. Things, by their very existence, cause stress because things must be maintained. The minute you accumulate something, the second law of thermodynamics comes into effect. That law states that everything is in a state of deterioration. Therefore, since everything we own will eventually need repair, more of our attention and time and energy are required to maintain our possessions. The more we have, the more our possessions have of us.

God's race changes our attitude about things. Running with God forces us either to lighten the load, slow the pace, or discontinue the race. Running causes us to focus on the goal—an abiding relationship with our energy source, God—rather than concentrating on peripheral roadside distractions.

When I was in the eighth grade I went out for junior varsity football. Things were going great until the day the varsity coach brought into our squad several who had been cut from the varsity squad, but still wanted to play. I was thirteen, and most of these boys were older. I was skinny and inexperienced, trying to compete against bigger, faster, more experienced boys. I became discouraged and quit.

I really wanted to play football. So the next year I set a simple, attainable goal for myself. It was just to stay on the squad throughout the season. This time I had no intention of quitting. By staying with the team that year, I not only met my goal, but to my own surprise, I was selected for the travel squad on the varsity team. Even though I did not play much, I was a legitimate, contributing member of the team.

The third year my goal was to play in a few games, even if I was on the second string. I exercised all summer long. I built up my strength and endurance because I knew if I made the second string, I would get some playing time. Two weeks into practice, the fellow in my position on the first team quit. As a sophomore I took his place and started on the varsity football team. Perseverance, or patient endurance, paid off.

Never, Never, Never Give Up!

He had two sons. The older was responsible, loyal, and trustworthy; the younger, flighty, self-centered, and a sower of wild oats. The inevitable day came, as the father knew it would, when his young son demanded his portion of the inheritance. Then he was gone. And the father watched him walk down that dusty road; his back straight and proud, his head high and determined. Walking that path led away from the safety of home and the love of his father.

During those lonely days the father sought news of his son. Messengers brought reports of riotous living in a far country, how he had squandered the estate, his dignity, his position, his health. They told of famine, poverty, and pigpens. And while the boy wallowed with the swine and tried to fill his empty stomach with their garbage, the father patiently waited—waited for him to come to his senses.

Then one day, from a great distance, he spotted him. There was the son coming down that dusty road, on his way back home. Matted hair, rags on his back, sores on his skin, but his father knew this was his child. And while the boy was still a long way off, his loving father watched him laboriously maneuver his tired, weary body down that familiar road. In a voice that sounded weak but pitifully familiar, the boy began to cry out, "I am no longer worthy to be your son . . . but I will forever be your servant. Father! Please! Let me come home" (see Luke 15:1–32). Overcome by love, the father began to run. Hurriedly, he rushed to his child, put his arms around his neck, and wept as he kissed him over and over and over again, welcoming him back to the safety of home.

The Father has seen us run through life. He watched as we walked away from Him. He has seen our plight as we tried to make it on our own. He knows that sometimes we get too tired to keep running. When that happens, when we do not think we can move another muscle or take another step closer to Him—that is when He runs to us. There in the dust of your race God comes and gives the strength to make it home.

After World War II, Winston Churchill, the man some claim saved the Western world from Nazi terror, was asked to come to his old high school and speak to a postwar graduating class. What would he say? This man had stood in the gap during the dark days of World War II when Great Britain endured alone against Hitler. Outnumbered, outgunned, yet he had encouraged Britain to persist in their cause.

Churchill's introduction took some time as the host repeated his many notable accomplishments. Then, Churchill himself walked to the podium. He looked at the young men before him and said, "Never give up! Never give up! Never, never, never give up." And he sat down.

Those are our instructions too. We cannot, we must not quit. Our goal is not to compete but to complete the race. Our task is not to place, but to finish. To finish is to win the gold medal. So, we run!

Many have gone before us and are now watching to see whether we faithfully complete the course. Should we not lay aside anything that encumbers us, take the weights off, get rid of the excess baggage, and ignore the comments of the crowds along the side of the road? Is it not time to run?

We cannot slow down and become entangled in the quicksand of this sinful world. We cannot let the glitter draw us aside. We look straight ahead at Jesus, the author, perfecter, and completer of faith. We stay on course and run with endurance—straight into the arms of God.

See His outstretched arms. Listen to His voice calling, "Come to Me, all who are weary and heavy-laden [have run to the point of exhaustion] and I will give you rest" (Matt. 11:28).

THREE

Flying on Eagle's Wings

The eagle that soars near the sun
Is not concerned
How it will cross the raging stream.[1]

In 1971, I was in Newport, Rhode Island, attending Naval Officer's Candidate School. While there I discovered that I was being considered for Naval Aviator's School.

It seemed like a great opportunity. Momentarily, I had grand illusions of soaring through the sky, commanding my own plane, charting my own course. I could picture myself flying, Red Baron style, into a glowing sunset with goggles adjusted, scarf waving in the breezes, women and children cheering as I flew off into the wild blue yonder to defend the cause of liberty.

Then I came to myself and started asking some questions.

"What kind of plane will I be flying?" I inquired.

"Why, the best plane in the force, the F-14 Tomcat. And we'll teach you to take off from the flight deck of an aircraft carrier," was the reply.

"An aircraft carrier? That postage-stamp-sized ship bobbing up and down out there . . . in all that ocean?"

"That's right," came the response.

I continued, "And I suppose you want me to fly that Tomcat over North Vietnam, where the inhabitants are doing everything except throwing rocks to knock F-14s out of the sky?"

"That pretty well sums it up, sailor," was the retort.

"Then, I'd have to fly back over the Pacific, find that bobbing, floating postage stamp, and land that plane—all by myself?"

"It's a chance of a lifetime, all right. Son, we're offering you the opportunity to fly. What about it?" Then he stood there grinning, anxiously anticipating my answer.

"No thanks," I said, as I hurriedly left the room.

At that time in my life the idea of flying did not appeal to me because I was not ready to make the commitment or take the risk. To fly would have meant extending my time in the armed services. To fly meant taking a chance on getting shot down, being a prisoner of war, or worse, maybe even being killed. So I weighed the benefits against the disadvantages and decided that I did not want to be a naval aviator. I chose not to fly.

Some have chosen not to fly; that is, they have chosen not to fly spiritually with God. They seem content to be spiritually grounded, complacently walking, sometimes venturing to run, but only when a crisis develops and life necessitates it. Bible study and prayer time are concepts they understand but do not personally enjoy doing; yet, they feel guilty when they do not at least go through the motions. The joy they once experienced in Christian life has been replaced by the legalism of walking . . . walking . . . walking. The psalmist cried out in his despair, "Restore to me the joy of Thy salvation, and sustain me with a willing spirit" (Ps. 51:12).

Essentially, David expressed what most Christians have felt at some point. "Oh God, give me back the gladness, the cheerfulness, the brightness that I once experienced in my salvation. The world slipped in and took Your place and now the laughter is gone, and I feel so empty. Help me stand fast, Father; and give me a willing, rational understanding of what 'standing fast' involves."

I Didn't Know I Had It in Me!

You see, most of life seems to involve walking . . . not flying. Walking is the logical way to travel short distances. It can be done through sheer discipline and the steely determination to move by putting one foot in front of another until we reach our destination. Walking assists us in accomplishing routine goals, those daily activities that demand our regular attention. However, while the ability to walk through life has its benefits, if it is our exclusive means of traveling from one place to another, it can become humdrum, tiresome, and time consuming.

Running, on the other hand, demands a specific goal. We run with a purpose in mind. There is an urgent task to complete, a definite time schedule to meet, a passion to finish the race. We run for joy, love, anger, hatred—for running is deeply emotional. Every fiber of our being is involved in running. It begins with a burning desire in the heart that heightens the resolve of the mind to accomplish a goal. Then, the body accelerates into high gear in order to attempt the run. Running takes us farther and quicker, but running for long periods of time, without an external energy source, can be exhausting, both physically and spiritually.

I once heard a story about a woodpecker. It seems he went through life much as the other woodpeckers, bouncing from tree to tree, drilling holes, searching for grubs, occasionally running from a hungry cat. He was comfortable.

Then it happened! One afternoon, as he was going about his business of boring into tree trunks—suddenly, unexpectedly, without announcement or warning—a bolt of lightning zapped that tree, splitting it right down the middle. The poor woodpecker was thrown several feet into the air and out over the forest. When he landed, he was belly up on the forest floor. He slowly opened his eyes. Dazed, feathers smoking, beak tingling, he shook himself. As he surveyed the demise of the mighty oak, he rubbed his smoldering beak and raised a skeptical eyebrow. Then, he stood straight up, thrust out his charred chest feathers, and strutted off through the woods saying, "My, I didn't know I had that in me!"

How many Christians are like that woodpecker? We spend our appointed days in the doldrums of the ordinary, frightened by the unscheduled, content to walk in the familiar, well-worn ruts of life. Then suddenly, God intervenes in our lives, moves us out of the mundane, changes our routine, lifts us above the forest floor for a brief moment—by doing something which takes us totally by surprise—and we look at our smoking beaks, dust ourselves off, and say, "Did I do that? I didn't know I had it in me."

We do not! That is flying. And flying takes an intervention from God. There is nothing within our physical being that will ever outfit us to fly spiritually. It takes supernatural ability. Flying enables us to leave the ground, to rise above circumstances, to view our world from a different perspective. And the only way we will ever accomplish that is by accessing a lift from God. That lift will empower us to soar beyond the limitations we have set for ourselves, to see things from God's point of view, and to understand where we fit into His kingdom plan.

I remember visiting Lucerne, Switzerland, and boarding a cable car headed up one of those dangerously beautiful mountain ranges in the Alps. As we were seated and left the ground, the air was weighty with humidity and heat. The sounds of the city were all around us; cars honking their horns for safe passing, children yelling and arguing in their play, discourteous street vendors hawking their wares. But as we were lifted above those surroundings, the climate became cool and peaceful, and we were able to see all those irritations as minor distractions . . . until they were completely out of sight, replaced by the splendid scenery of the mountains. Isaiah 40:31 proclaims, "Those who wait for the LORD will gain new strength; they will mount up with wings like eagles." We can experience that lift from God.

Poetically, Isaiah encourages us to exchange our "strength," or abilities, for God's, sprout our spiritual eagle's wings, lock them into place—and fly. In the flying, we confirm our trust in God and exchange our weakness for His great strength. The thought carries with it the idea of exchanging old worn out garments for new ones. In Romans 13:14, Paul says the same thing when he encourages us to "put on the Lord Jesus Christ, and make no provision for the flesh in regard to its lusts." And in Colossians 3:10, we read, "Put on the new self who is being renewed, to a true knowledge according to the image of the One who created him."

See! We can fly!

You see, a person can be abandoned, beaten, betrayed, crucified—dead and buried in a tomb just as our Lord was—but when men and women learn the secret of flying, they cannot be bound by the natural law of gravity. A greater law takes over: the law of aerodynamics.

"Do you really want to fly?" That is the question.

Apart from the supernatural, Holy Spirit power of God in our lives, we will never fly. The decision is ours. Are we going to spend the rest of our lives walking five or six feet from the earth's surface, incapacitated by every storm cloud that happens to hang over our head? There comes a point in our life when we, like a giant 747 aircraft, have to decide whether or not to take off. We are moving down the runway, picking up speed—and now have to decide, if we are going to decrease power, slow down, and head back to the terminal or give it full throttle and fly.

Certainly, the weather looks stormy at times. The wind is blowing. The clouds may cause us to experience some turbulence. But we are at the point of no return. To keep going and fail to take off will be disastrous. Take off! Our greater danger is not that our aim is too high and we miss it, but that it is too low and we reach it. We need to fly! When we break through beyond the fog and vapors of this world, we will see the Son.

What Keeps You from Flying?

No matter how motivated or well equipped, some birds just do not fly. The ostrich is the largest of all birds with all the characteristics of being a bird: feathers, wings, a beak, and it lays eggs—but it does not fly. Throughout the Bible this bird is mentioned several times but seldom in a favorable light.

The Book of Job gives us some insight into the nature of this flightless bird (see Job 39:13–18). First, Job calls attention to the large, powerless wings of the weighty ostrich. However, he never mentions their incapacity for flight, only the fact that the birds strut around flaunting their lovely white plumage, flapping their wings "joyously," but never attempting to take off (v. 13). The marketability of those lovely plumes is responsible for many of those birds being hunted and killed.

Next, Job refers to the female's incapacity to care for her young (vv. 14–16). Oddly enough, since she is a ground dweller, her eggs are simply deposited, along with several other females' eggs, in the same nest, which is little more than a hollow scooped in the sand. During the daytime the frivolous females simply cover the eggs with sand to conceal them from predators and leave them to be hatched at the mercy of the warm desert sunbeams. Even though the eggs are buried about a foot below the surface, they are vulnerable to scavengers and the heavy foot of a casual passerby. When hatched, the young are left mainly to fend for themselves, since the parent bird has no method of self-defense on the wide sandy desert except great speed, which is also possessed by the hatchling (v. 18).

Job also reflects on the bird's seeming stupidity (v. 17). Since she consistently relies on instinct, not intellect, the ostrich is predictable even to her enemies. Her habit is to always run against the wind in order to catch a scent of an approaching assailant. Observing this pattern, her foes develop strategies, and eventually she is subdued. The ostrich lacks discernment. She will eat any substance, even those that cannot be used for food. Knives, bits of bone, and metal, even bullets hot from the mold, have been retrieved from the digestive systems of these birds.

Too Much Weight

Some Christians are like the flightless ostrich. They have become too heavy to take off because of the excess weight of this world. They are "encumbered," weighted down because of the bulk or mass, the heaviness of life (Heb. 12:1).

Luke recorded an account where Jesus was an invited dinner guest at the home of "one of the leaders of the Pharisees" (Luke 14:1). Everyone sat down, anxious to hear what this renegade prophet had to say. Jesus, the master storyteller, began telling a poignant parable. "A certain man," he said, "was giving a big dinner, and he invited many; and at the dinner hour he sent his slave to say to those who had been invited, 'Come; for everything is ready now.' But they all alike began to make excuses" (Luke 14:16–18).

One had bought a piece of land and begged to be excused so he could go look at it. His possessions weighed him down. Another had purchased five yoke of oxen and needed to try them out to see if he had made a good business deal. His career weighed him down. The third fellow informed his host that he had married a wife; therefore, with no further explanation, he asked to be excused. He was weighted down by interpersonal and family relationships.

Without exception, each man who had accepted an invitation to dine with the host asked to be excused, using flimsy reasons for not showing up—even after the host had gone to the trouble of preparing the meal and sending for them. Of those presumptuous ones, Jesus said, "None of those men who were invited shall taste of my dinner" (Luke 14:24).

What about us? Have we accumulated so much of this world's weight that we find it inconvenient, maybe even impossible, to respond to the invitation of God? Anything can weigh us down: religion, possessions, occupation, relationships. Even our own personal comfort can keep us from experiencing the abundant feast of life that God has prepared.

It is said that a certain society in South Africa once wrote to David Livingstone: "Have you found a good road to where you are? If so, we want to know how to send other men to join you." Livingstone replied: "If you have men who will come *only* if they know there is a good road, I *don't want them.* I want men who will come if there is *no* road at all."[2] Do not let anything keep you from doing what God has called you to do! The apostle Paul admonishes us to strive for and accumulate a different type of weight, "For momentary, light affliction is producing for us an eternal weight of glory far beyond all comparison" (2 Cor. 4:17).

Too Much Clutter

Spiritual flying is also obstructed when Christians concentrate too much attention on those things that distract from the goal of getting into the air. Even though Christians, like the ostrich, seem fully equipped to fly, something keeps them grounded. Perhaps it is the time-consuming business of picking up the "me deep" litter—the problems, the needs, the hurts—of our lives. That part of us can block God, as well as others from our lives, until there is nothing left but "me."

We will not fly with God as long as we are riveted to the ground by the "me deep" litter of what might have been, what has been, or what will be. The people in our lives, the events that have taken place, and the trauma we may have experienced cannot keep us down unless we allow it. Isaiah 40:29 encourages us to throw off the past and rise above our circumstances because "He gives strength to the weary, and to him who lacks might He increases power."

Our tendency is to blame our flightless behavior on something or someone else. "Oh, God," we cry. "I'm down because of what my parents did to me as a child." Or, "I'm discouraged in my job." Or, "I'm weary in trying to deal with my children." Or, "I'm angry about the way I am treated by my spouse." Isaiah explained, "God has already given, He is giving, and He will continue to give all that we need in order to rise above our circumstances and fly." That Hebrew word "give" means "add to, appoint or apply." God can take what little vitality we have left and add to it, supplying what is lacking, in order for us to take off.

It is hard to hear God, to sense God, and to believe God with so much interference. Sometimes, knowing that God is there for you is realized only when you push the debris aside and take time to be alone with Him, acknowledging His presence.

Moses, in preparation for leading God's people out of Egypt, had been placed—not by choice, but by God—on the back side of the desert tending his father-in-law's sheep. There, God purged him of Egyptian influences and taught him desert survival techniques. One day his concentration shifted from the flock he was shepherding and the terrain that had become his prison, up . . . up . . . up the side of Mt. Horeb. There he noticed, for the first time, the bush that burned with a message from God and yet was not consumed. I wonder how long that bush had to burn before Moses pushed aside every outside interference, got quiet, and finally looked up to hear from God?

Just like that ostrich, we can run across the hot deserts of our lives, throwing out our wings for no other reason than to show the scars and scream, "Look what life has done to us!" Or we can use those wings for the purpose they were created— to fly.

Fear of the Unknown

Some Christians do not fly because they have always walked—and they are unwilling to change. We get in spiritual ruts, in paths carved by someone else, and there we anchor ourselves. We look for security in a certain location, another person, a job, a house, a church, a pastor; then, when something causes that temporal world to crumble, we crumble along with it.

One of the most basic needs in life is security. Now, our concept of security is probably preserving the status quo, maintaining control; in other words, we continue to walk rather than learn a new skill, like flying. When we talk about spiritual flying, we are talking about giving up control. This is the first step in getting off the ground. God is not interested in seeing us hobble around hanging on to self-made "control crutches." Clinging to those burdensome crutches immobilizes the Christian and makes it impossible to move in any direction. God wants to see us fly, and because of that, sometimes it means spiritually kicking the control crutches out from under us. Probably the greatest single barrier to flying is the fear of leaving the familiar and launching out into God's unknown—by faith.

When God called me to seminary, I was pastoring a little church in eastern Kentucky. The "holy gnawing" began that would eventually point me toward Louisville, Kentucky, and The Southern Baptist Theological Seminary. I was very uncomfortable with the direction God was leading. "Why upset the apple cart at this junction in my life, Lord? I'm twenty-nine years old, a family man . . . my church is growing. Why me? Why now?" I asked.

Those are significant questions, and they will identify the man or woman who refuses to give God control. You see, God is ever working to move us beyond specific locations—those areas in our lives where we seem to have pinned Him down—toward the real security of a personal relationship and trust in Him. He is ever teaching us that we are pilgrims in this world—just quickly passing through— using, but not hoarding or clinging, to the "entangling things" (Heb. 12:1).

Jesus' technique was to send His disciples into the world with an assigned task, remove the artificial props, and not hand out emergency numbers (see Matt. 10:16). He still does that today. His purpose is to make us totally dependent on God, totally independent of man-made crutches. He blocks off emergency exits, knowing our tendency to take the easy way out. He seals up all the doors, burns all the bridges—except the one that leads to God.

Jamie Buckingham tells the story of meeting a Roman Catholic priest. It seems the priest was working in the most miserable of situations, the slums of Bangkok. He lived in an animal slaughterhouse. During the day he spent most of his time with the people. At night he slept in a tiny corner. Buckingham remembers: "The smell was abominable. The conditions too ghastly to describe."[3] On one particular day the priest escorted him around, showing the places where he worked and introducing his Thai friends.

Buckingham finally stopped him. "Father, where are you from?"

The priest looked at him in amazement. "I'm from Bangkok."

"No," Buckingham said, "I mean, where is your home?"

"Oh, now I understand," he said with a smile. "I was born in Portland, Oregon. I went to college in Oregon and seminary in Chicago. But I'm from Bangkok. This is my place."

"No wonder," thought Buckingham, "he could sleep in that stinking slaughterhouse. He had found his place . . . not in Bangkok, but in God."[4]

Are we ready to allow God to control our lives? If we keep clutching for control, we will end up like that silly ostrich, always running . . . running . . . running in the same direction. The enemies of God have easily figured out that simple strategy, and if we continue that tactic they will remain close on our heels. The only way to escape the danger is to allow God to pull us out of the ruts, change our course, and give us the power to fly.

Have you ever wanted to do something different, something you have not done before . . . to the glory of God? Of course, there is an element of risk involved. At first, until we learn to trust the Lord, flying is frightening . . . because we are no longer in control. The Lord, our Guide, makes all the decisions: which route to take, how high to fly, whether to go around the storm, through it, or above it. When flying, He has all authority and once we are in the air we do not land until we reach our destination—by the way, He decides that too.

Some birds do not fly; some Christians will not. It is because they are like that misguided ostrich, pecking first here, then there, consuming everything and anything this world has to offer, unable to discern what is digestible and what is not. They eat and become full, but they are never nutritionally satisfied. They eat and become full, but the garbage of this world has no taste to the Christian. They eat and become full, but spend their nights tossing and turning with heavenly heartburn . . . there's no rest, no peace.

Two artists were commissioned to paint a picture representing their idea of peace. The first one drew an idyllic scene. He painted an ocean, still as a pond, reflecting each line and curve of the sailboat drifting effortlessly over it. Overhead the blue sky was flecked with fluffy white clouds. On the shore children played happily as they built sand castles. This scene represented peace to the first artist.

The second artist painted a picture closer to reality. His painting revealed a savage and rocky shore where angry waves crashed against the coast in towering clouds of spray. A storm loomed on the horizon, and the sky was dark and foreboding. Yet, far up on a rocky crag, almost hidden in a cleft of the rock, sat a bird, safe and secure in her nest, sheltered from the wind. There she sat, looking out with a serene and untroubled eye at all the turmoil beneath. This was a picture of peace indeed.

Sometimes the Lord calms the storm; sometimes He lets the storm rage and calms His children. This kind of peace is available to you. Jesus said, "Ask, and it shall be given to you; seek, and you shall find; knock, and it shall be opened to you. For everyone who asks receives, and he who seeks finds, and to him who knocks it shall be opened" (Matt. 7:7–8). Right now, simply call out to your loving heavenly Father. Whisper to Him that you are bored with walking and tired of running. Ask Him for wings . . . and prepare to fly.

Some Birds Soar

Not all birds are like the ostrich; some soar. When Isaiah penned the words, "Yet those who wait for the LORD will gain new strength; they will mount up with wings like eagles," he must have had a picture in his mind. He had spent time in the desert, and there no doubt he had observed the eagle in flight. Isaiah watched the bird position itself on a high cliff, wait for the wind, slip from the edge, spread those magnificent wings, and with very little effort catch the thermal updrafts that are so common in the desert. The superheated air from the desert floor creates updrafts that will ascend thousands of feet. Isaiah had seen the eagle rise, higher and higher, effortlessly using those thermals as a source of power . . . soaring where no other bird dared go.

With this in mind and knowing the hardships the Israelites faced as they left their life of slavery in Babylon and traveled back to Jerusalem, Isaiah looked at that ragtag crew and wrote, "Some of you will need the strength just to walk and not become weary; God will provide it. Others of you will be able to move faster; yet you will need strength from God to run and not get tired. But a few of you will make the trip by soaring—catching the thermals and flying in strength and power, utilizing the wind of God."

Now, we know the human body is not fashioned in such a way that it is literally capable of flight. That is impossible. Spiritual flight is the subject of this chapter and it has to do with attitude. It is being equipped to experience the abundant Christian life regardless of the situation. It is the ability to live above circumstances, rather than underneath them. It is being able to pull people up, rather than allowing yourself to be pulled down.

If you are secretly expressing the desire to fly, think about the eagle. Does he expend great amounts of energy in order to soar? Is it necessary for him to furiously flap those powerful wings to lift himself? No! He simply takes advantage of the resource available to him. It is the *ruach*, the wind.

When the Old Testament, desert-dwelling Jew heard the wind howling, he called it the *ruach,* the mighty wind. Interestingly enough, the same word was used by King David to describe the Holy Spirit of God (the breath of God), when he wrote, "Take not thy *Ruach* from me" (Ps. 51:11). At Pentecost, when the Holy Spirit of God was poured out on believers, the experience was described as sounding like a thunderous, "violent, rushing *Pnoe*" (a blowing breath). Again, here the wind is synonymous with the Spirit of God. When Elijah stood on the mountain waiting for the Lord to pass by, God did not speak to Elijah in the great storm, the earthquake, or by fire. God spoke to Elijah in "a sound of a gentle blowing" (1 Kings 19:12). It is easy to understand from these passages that the "breath of God" (the Holy Spirit) fills—blows spiritual life into—God's children thus lifting them from within.

Like that eagle, who catches the mighty desert wind and travels so high that ice sometimes forms on his wings, you can catch hold of the mighty Spirit of God and draw upon His power. The Holy Spirit is the tremendous power of God alive and active in our world today. When we wait on Him, He teaches us how to fly with God. He lives within every believer and He equips us to do the impossible—if He is not hindered. He is the link between heaven and earth, between God and man. That link is interrupted by prayerlessness. There is no power without prayer. There is no power unless we maintain a steady diet of nutrition from the Word of God.

"But how can I know the power is really available for me?" you may ask.

Living and experiencing are the double majors at the "University of the Power of God." The only way you will graduate and realize that power is to jump, by faith, headlong into life, trusting God to be your spiritual safety net. Andrew Murray said, "Receive what you do not comprehend, submit to what you cannot understand, accept and expect what to reason appears a mystery, believe what looks impossible, walk in a way which you know not . . . such are the first lessons in the school of God."[5]

Not until then will the power to fly be appropriated.

What Comes with the Power?

Renewal

I know a young lady, a senior social work major in a prominent Christian university. She is a believer in Christ who has dedicated her entire life to ministering to the hurting and broken people that God brings to her.

During her internship, she was assigned to work with AIDS patients, those ravaged by the cruel and relentless virus that never gives up until its victim does. Knowing that Christ was the center of her life, her advisors repeatedly warned her not to impose her Christian beliefs on the ones with whom she worked.

One night she was called to the bedside of a man whose body was so wasted that she was fearful his bones might puncture the thin layer of skin that covered them. Because he was convulsing, she realized his life was slipping away. She knew there was little she could do except hold his hand and pray, so she decided to sit with him through the night hours. In the wee hours of the morning he began to tearfully share bits and pieces of his life, a life lived outside the grace and forgiveness of a merciful Savior. He spoke of dying and his insurmountable fear.

It was too much for the young woman. She began to share with him the unconditional love and acceptance of Jesus Christ. She told him that Jesus had helped her overcome her own fear of dying by promising eternal life. His eyes brightened as he realized he too could stand before God clean and unashamed, simply by asking Christ for forgiveness and salvation. There in the darkness of a room where the unyielding presence of death hovered, she tenderly clutched his hand in hers and watched the light of Jesus infiltrate his heart as they prayed together; he finally found peace.

For her there was a reprimand, a severe warning never to do it again, and threats of retaliation when her grades were posted. But that was a small price to pay . . . for flying.

Another place, another time, another man stood naked on the shores of the Sea of Galilee, beating his chest, cursing and terrorizing any unsuspecting fishermen who mistakenly ventured too close to the coastline. On his body were the marks of man-made chains and shackles, scars placed there by his frightened countrymen in a vain attempt to subdue the raging spirits that tormented him.

His beastly keen eyes had watched the disciples' boat as it approached his secluded portion of the beach. A strange, unsettling stir ran up his backbone as Jesus left the ship and walked toward the demoniac's dwelling place among the tombs. With a horrifying scream expressing the pain of a hundred nights spent lying alone in those caves of death, he lunged toward Jesus, breathless and exhausted, saliva mingled with earth running down his tangled beard, spent by the demons tearing him apart from within.

And there, in a heap on the ground, he came to the end of himself. Tough exterior gone, totally out of strength, he dropped down, cut and bleeding before Jesus.

That was when the voices started, a legion of them, chanting a demonic chorus that grew louder and louder until it was finally drowned out by the thunderous roar of two thousand pigs running, wildly running, to drown their misery in the sea.

With just a word from Jesus, the demonic forces were gone, and a restless spirit was renewed. And when the curious crowds came to gawk, they "observed the man who had been demon-possessed sitting down, clothed and in his right mind" (Mark 5:15).

Like that man, "you were dead in your trespasses and sins. But God, being rich in mercy, because of His great love with which He loved us, even when we were dead in our transgressions, made us alive together with Christ (by grace you have been saved)" (Eph. 2:1,4–5).

Relationship

God not only renews us, but He also brings us into a relationship with Him. Just as he initiated and developed a relationship with the demon-possessed man, He wants to do the same for us. That relationship is not merited on account of good looks, superior talents, or dynamic personality. A relationship with God is based entirely on "the kind intention of His will" (Eph. 1:5). It pleases God when the relationship is based on fellowship and trust.

The analogy of an eagle with its young was used by Moses to describe the desired relationship between God and Israel when he said, "Like an eagle that stirs up its nest, that hovers over its young, He spread His wings and caught them, He carried them on His pinions" (Deut. 32:11).

Desert dwellers had watched the eagle build her nest high on a jagged cliff, hanging it precariously from the side of the steep precipice where no predator could endanger the young. Once built, the nest was lined with the mother's own feathers as a soft mattress for the eggs, then the hatchlings. The observers had seen the mother bird spend most of her time supplying food for her voracious eaglets. This seemingly endless process continued during the birds' period of rapid growth.

Then one day the adult eagle did a surprising thing. She came to the nest not to nourish, but to nurture. One at a time, she shoved each bird to the edge and unceremoniously pushed them out. Down the face of the mountain tumbled the shrieking eaglet, its immature wings flapping furiously. But just before it hit the hard terrain below, the mother eagle swooped under her baby, allowed him to clutch at her feathers with his tiny talons, and back to the nest they returned—only to repeat the procedure over and over again until his wings matured and he was able to fly solo.

In the relationship between God and His children, our heavenly Father not only nourishes, but He also nurtures. Nurturing involves flight training that takes place right now in our lives. God uses that situation in our life that has us completely perplexed, bewildered, and confused, to teach us how to fly with Him. That's right! With Him. We are not out there midway between heaven and earth alone. We may feel as if we are in a spiraling free-fall, but He is underneath us, giving us support, ready to catch us before we crash. Faith is the talon by which our souls cling to God. We need to catch hold of Him and hang on; He's teaching us to fly.

Release

When we are released we have developed the expertise to leave the confines of our comfortable nests to fly. No longer is it necessary for God to push and nudge; we are now anxious and able to get about His business. The demon-possessed man, realizing that Jesus was leaving, became anxious and began "entreating Him that he might accompany Him" (Mark 5:18). But the Lord released him to serve in a different way, not by going but by staying. "Go home to your people and report to them what great things the Lord has done for you, and how He had mercy on you," Jesus told him (Mark 5:19).

Years ago an old Indian found an eagle egg. He took that egg and placed it in the nest of a prairie chicken, curious to learn if it would hatch. When the eagle egg did indeed hatch, the mother prairie chicken noticed that the young bird looked different, acted different, and sounded different; but, as far as she knew, he was her chick; consequently he was raised as a prairie chicken.

Like his adopted brothers and sisters, he learned to peck around on the ground for his food. He thought prairie chicken thoughts and did prairie chicken activities. "You're a prairie chicken," said his mother. "You're a prairie chicken," said his father. And everything around him validated that fact.

Until one day he heard the call of a mighty eagle flying overhead. He looked up, mesmerized, and saw this bird flying higher and higher, until it disappeared, flying beyond the clouds.

"What was that?" he cried.

"Oh, that's an eagle," one of the prairie chickens longingly answered.

"Man," said the prairie chicken (who was really an eagle). "I sure wish I could fly like that." And with a sigh, he shook his head and went back to pecking and scratching.

Have you been conditioned to believe you are a prairie chicken? Have the choices you made somewhere back in life placed you in the wrong nest and permanently grounded you? God says, "Spread your wings." Exchange that prairie chicken tag for one that reads *eagle* and fly in the strength of God.

Winning the Daily Battles

Battle fatigue is caused by a tiring tour of duty. Its symptoms include weariness, severe exhaustion, and a mental tiredness that stifles creative abilities. It manifests itself when a soldier is placed in a position where he performs the same job over and over again without rest. It makes little difference whether the assignment is honorable or menial. Battle fatigue becomes noticeable when the routine becomes too commonplace, the rewards and recreation are absent, and there is no promise of relief.

A soldier stretched mentally, physically, and emotionally is like an elongated rubber band or a tightly wound coil, ready to snap with the slightest touch.

Regretfully, the battlefield is not always located on foreign soil but is frighteningly close at hand. Sounds of war emanate daily from the lives of Christians, as well as non-Christians, all across our nation. Men and women are warring against each other in the confines of their homes, shedding emotional and sometimes physical blood, and generating scars that disfigure them as well as the little ones who first watch the battle from a distance and then eventually join it as conflict inevitably develops between parent and child.

The workplace has become a battlefield as coworkers jockey for position and power while they climb that proverbial career ladder to success. Complicated relationships develop within families as inlaws and "outlaws" demand valuable space, limited time, and exhausted energy. Neighbors hurl emotionally charged hand grenades across backyard fences while watching their communities deteriorate in crime and moral decay. Sometimes it all becomes too much. The sights, the sounds, the emotions elicited by the battle—the daily grind—flood us with the sensation of hopeless desperation and force us to surrender in the face of all this overpowering stimuli.

How does life, which starts out uncomplicated and with such promise, end in battle fatigue? What are the dynamics that lead to isolation, separation, and exasperation? The sworn enemy to overcoming the daily hurdles of life is an apathetic attitude. That attitude is brought on by an absence of personal priorities coupled with severe relational overdrive.

Apathy is a malignant relational cancer that develops over a period of time. If left unchecked and untreated it can infiltrate every aspect of life: marriage, home, community, and career. In its wake, the passion, excitement, and enthusiasm that once permeated life is lost. In its worst form it leaves its victims disinterested and unconcerned, merely existing from one day to the next—"getting by"—with no joy for the wonderful adventure of living.

The second part of this book, "Winning the Daily Battles," is designed to help you overcome by showing you strategies for managing lifestyle areas often affected by apathy.

FOUR

Developing Personal Priorities

He who reigns within himself,
and rules passions, desires, and fears,
is more than a king.[1]

In the children's story, *The Adventures of Alice in Wonderland,* Alice comes to a junction in the road. She asks her friend, the Cheshire Cat, for advice. "Cheshire, would you tell me please, which way I ought to go from here?"

"That depends a good deal on where you want to go," said the cat.

"I don't care where," said Alice.

After the briefest pause, the cat replied, "Then it doesn't matter which way you go."

God Has a Plan for Your Life

That grinning make-believe cat was right. If we set out to travel but have no firm destination in mind, then any old road will do. In a children's story such spontaneous recklessness can initiate an adventure; but in real life, leaving the direction and the plan for reaching it to chance may lead to disaster.

God created you a spiritual being in a physical body so that His Spirit could reside in you, and eventually you could live eternally with Him in heaven: "'For I know the plans that I have for you, . . . 'plans for welfare and not for calamity to give you a future and a hope'" (Jer. 29:11). Therefore, where we are headed does make a great deal of difference. If our ultimate goal is heaven, then our primary aspiration in life will be to know and please God, who is responsible for the plan that will get us there.

In order to avoid directional chaos in life it is essential for the Christian to develop a standard of God-pleasing personal priorities. Balancing life's priorities clarifies direction and charts a reliable course that transports the believer closer to the safety of the Savior and farther from the dangerous quicksand of battle fatigue. However, folks do not have clear-cut directions or a workable plan for their lives. Most allow circumstances to dominate their schedules and dictate their attitudes. Here's a case in point:

Karen jumps out of bed at 5:30 A.M. feeling no more refreshed or rested than when she climbed into bed a few hours earlier. With a husband and three kids to get out of the house, she does not have a minute to spare. Hitting the floor running, she showers and prepares herself for the upcoming day. Down the stairs she hurries to fix breakfast for two ill-humored, school-age children whose only desire is to stay in their warm beds. "Honey, where's that report I worked on last night?" her husband shouts. "Mom, where's my homework? I left it on the table," her son complains.

She leaves the older children to catch the bus alone and she rushes off to the baby-sitter with her four-year-old daughter. There she must again encounter the clinging, the tears, the chronic guilt for walking out the door, and she hears her preschooler's childish voice pleading, "Mommy, please take me with you."

Work is hectic. Her company has downsized, and everyone is doing double duty. There is pressure to be productive. Demanding clients and customers create havoc with her schedule. Most of them deposit psychological baggage in her life, baggage she must deal with before she goes home.

Rush-hour traffic prolongs her day as she wearily picks up her daughter and rushes home. There she finds two latch-key kids arguing over which TV program to watch and a house that looks as if it has been hit by a hurricane.

The last thing she wants is to jump right into her second full-time job—that of caretaker-homemaker. She needs a moment of quiet because she is physically, emotionally, and psychologically drained. Yet the first question her oldest son asks when she walks in the door is, "What's for dinner?" Frustrated and baffled by the constant barrage of daily mortar fire, she slumps into a chair, shaking her head, not sure which direction she should run first. She is experiencing a classic case of twentieth-century "battle fatigue."

Putting Your World Back Together

A recent study of people who are self-proclaimed New York City yuppies yielded some interesting statistics. All reported six-figure yearly incomes. They lived in houses valued at a quarter of a million dollars. Ninety per cent collected art, and most of them went to Europe at least every other year.

The disturbing part of the research is that two out of five are under the regular care of a psychiatrist. One out of every two has gone through a divorce. Eight out of ten are estranged from their children. Three out of four are under the care of a physician for chronic depression. Four out of eight are addicted to cocaine. And one out of every five is under federal indictment for fraud. These people are the ones Louis Lapman of *Harper's* magazine suggests need a "cure of style." Their lifestyle has given them battle fatigue.

Is the American dream really a dream, or is it a nightmare? If we have not established a workable set of personal priorities—those consistent biblical life principles that bolster our determination to serve Christ and adhere to His precepts—our world of papier mâché and make-believe will not stand the tornado-force winds of life, even if we have established what seems to be a secure financial base. In this life a seemingly successful career and a bulging portfolio do not guarantee happiness or security. It takes more.

By nature, humans need and yearn for both spiritual and personal relationships that replenish emotional energy and give hope to persevere. It is therefore far more important to learn how to handle life and how to relate to people than how to manipulate finances, decorate houses, set the latest fashion trend, or cut a lucrative business deal. Jesus admonished us to be careful of priorities that cause us to concentrate only on accumulating temporal treasures upon earth. His advice was to "lay up for yourselves treasures in heaven . . . for where your treasure is, there will your heart be also" (Matt. 6:20–21).

Recently, I watched as a local television station reported a house fire. From the looks of things, the physical frame of the house and all its paraphernalia were totally destroyed. Yet standing there on the lawn in front of the burned-out remains of his house was a weathered old grandfather. With tears running down his cheeks, he softly spoke into the camera. "We lost everything we had in that house, but maybe someday we can replace all of that. You see, we got everything out that matters. We got all the little ones out of the fire." That man knew what was really important. Jobs, furniture, houses, automobiles, prestige, and affluence can all be lost in one moment and restored in the next, but you cannot replace people.

People Are Important

Kathy was lonely so she decided to go to a pet store and purchase an animal for companionship. While there the owner convinced her she needed a parrot that could talk. Excited about the prospect of owning a pet with whom she could communicate, she invested a large sum of money and took the bird home.

For a while, things went well, but then she noticed that the parrot had stopped talking. Kathy called the store to inquire about what she should do.

"Did you buy a mirror?" the store operator questioned.

"No," was Kathy's reply, "but I will if you think it might make my parrot talk again."

The mirror was purchased, but still there were no words. Only silence greeted her from the cage. In her disappointment Kathy went back to the store where she was informed that in order to talk a parrot needed exercise, such as running up and down a tiny ladder placed strategically within the cage. Then, surely, the words would follow. A ladder was added to the purchase list, but to no avail. At the end of the week she was back in the pet store demanding a refund. Her bird was still not talking.

"Perhaps," hypothesized the shrewd store owner, "your bird would talk if you purchased a swing and placed it in his cage. Birds do love to swing, you know." But even after the purchase of a swing there were no words from her fretting feathered friend.

Three days later Kathy stomped into the store, slammed the door, and demanded to see the owner. Hurrying into the room, he inquired about the voiceless parrot.

"He died this afternoon," she blurted out.

"He died! Did he ever talk?" asked the puzzled proprietor.

"Yes, he said a few words as he breathed his last," whimpered Alice pitifully.

"Well, what did he say?" coaxed the pet shop owner.

"He said, 'Don't they ever sell any food at that store?'" This story describes the dilemma of human existence. Twentieth-century folks are so busy making a life they do not have time to communicate or to incorporate into that life the details that make it worth living. Like that lady in the first part of this chapter whose life is continually in overdrive, we fill our days with things we deem "mandatory" and neglect the "essential." We work our bodies and minds to the point of exhaustion trying to provide mirrors and swings and ladders for ourselves and our loved ones—only to find that gadgets can never replace the true food of the soul: love and companionship. One of the primary causes of battle fatigue is that Christians neglect regarding the people God brings into their lives as priorities. Too often our priorities are material rather than spiritual or personal.

God's Plan for Success

The Christian life is often an enigma to those who are outside it. Words such as *success, influence, power, prosperity,* take on new and different meanings when used in context with Christ's teachings. R. D. Hitchcock made an interesting observation on the spiritual road to success when he said, "Every step in our progress toward success is a sacrifice. We gain by losing; grow by dwindling; live by dying."[2]

God's formula for success is all tied up in developing the same personal priorities as the saints written about within the pages of the Bible. Of His Word and the instructions found there, He says, "Meditate on it day and night, so that you may be careful to do according to all that is written in it; for then you will make your way prosperous, and then you will have success" (Josh. 1:8).

Discover God's plan for your life and set out to accomplish it. God's plan for us is to be successful by His standards, not by the standards established by the world. In His Word He has given many examples of people who set out on a pathway to establish personal priorities in their lives and thus became successful according to God's standard of measurement.

Nowhere in Scripture is this concept more evident than in the life of John the Baptist. Clothed in a garment of camel's hair held together only by the leather belt around his waist, he made his meals of locust and wild honey. He openly challenged the sterile, legalistic religious system of his day. He baptized in the Jordan River, encouraging men and women to change their hearts before they attempted to change their habits.

John was an imposing, charismatic figure who could have capitalized on his popularity among the common people and elevated himself to a position of leadership, even messiah-ship. But he did not attempt to seize control because, first and foremost, his priorities were in order. He knew what he was supposed to be doing, and he set out to do that and that alone, without unnecessarily adding to his job description. He knew his job was to set the stage for the Messiah. He was the forerunner, the warm-up act, the one to prepare this planet for the advent of God "in the flesh."

In order to avoid personal battle fatigue we need to prioritize just as John did. Yet often we do just the opposite, pumping our prestige, padding our power base by doing things God never intended for us to do. That is like the story I heard about the bank president who admitted he was working himself to death. When questioned, "Whose work are you doing right now?" his reply was, "Well, to be honest, the cashier's."[3] John the Baptist knew who he was, and what it was that God wanted him to do. Because he had an ongoing fellowship with the Father, he never once attempted to function in the area where only Jesus was qualified to labor.

Remain flexible enough to make directional adjustments. By establishing and adhering to the personal priorities in his life, John was able to remain flexible. He was able to make directional adjustments when God's greater plan required it. For example, he had told the crowd, "After me comes a Man who has a higher rank than I" (John 1:30). Yet when Jesus, the high-ranking One, submitted Himself to John for baptism, he initially refused before he corrected his spiritual perspective and complied with the Savior's request.

On another occasion (see John 1:37), John watched as his disciples left him one by one to follow Jesus. He knew he was seeing the beginning of the end of his short-lived earthly acclaim. While his flesh may have cried out for more, his spirit had the proper perspective when he acknowledged, "He who has the bride is the bridegroom; but the friend of the bridegroom, who stands and hears him, rejoices greatly because of the bridegroom's voice. And so this joy of mine has been made full. He must increase, but I must decrease" (John 3:29–30).

Christians intent on establishing personal priorities in their lives must remain flexible, always ready and willing to change their direction when it interferes with God's greater plan for their lives. A highly motivated insurance salesman had been told by his boss that he was not assertive enough. Wanting to prove his demanding boss wrong, the salesman noticed a scaffold outside his seventeenth-floor office window lined with workmen. He made a sign asking the workmen if they would be interested in life, accident, or disability insurance and held it up to the window where they could see it clearly. Within a few minutes a message came down the line. "We will talk to you about insurance, but you have to join us on the scaffold." He did and sold over $50,000 worth of insurance that very day. When he changed his perspective, he was able to accomplish his goal of selling insurance.

That is what Christians intent on following God's direction must do: view life from a different perspective—God's. Then we remain flexible, willing to take a chance and climb out on a limb with God, without complaining about His methods or criticizing His motives. Being positive, optimistic, and encouraging while allowing God to make necessary heavenly adjustments and holy alterations is one sign that God is the main priority in our life.

I will never forget the wonderful story about Booker T. Washington, a man who had developed impeccable priorities in his life. On one occasion he arrived in a certain city to make a very important speech. Knowing his train had arrived late, and realizing the importance of his mission, he hailed a taxi cab. When the surly driver arrived he growled, "I don't drive black men." To which the great man, Washington, replied, "All right then, get in the back. I'll drive you."

In life the tendency is to do it the way we have always done it, to follow the path of least resistance, the well-traveled path. But God is not nearly as concerned with a comfortable path as He is that we reach our prescribed destination. Sometimes God deliberately changes our path to change our perspective and our priorities. Many times it is those deliberate changes that enable us to accomplish the greatest and most noble missions to which He has called us.

Manage your motives and adjust your attitude. Motives (why you do what you do) and attitude (how we feel about what we do) are keys to avoiding battle fatigue. John the Baptist realized his earthly ministry was to be short-lived. His life was just an exclamation point on the pages of history. But he also had an understanding of its significance in God's long-range plan and its eternal ramifications for generations to come. That is why he could go to his death with as much vigor as when he dipped sinners into the muddy waters of the Jordan. His personal motive was clearly to serve God, and that he did, whether in the fresh winds of the desert or deep in the putrid dungeon where he faced his executioners.

In a cathedral in Milan there are three different signs over three different doors. The sign above the right door says All That Pleases Is but for a Moment. The sign over the left door reads All That Troubles Is but for a Moment. The center door displays this thought-provoking sign That Only Is Important

Which Is Eternal. John had already chosen the center door, and so must the person who desires to establish godly priorities in his life.

Proper motives and appropriate attitudes lead to personal serenity and spiritual blessing—even when circumstances seem hopeless.

John the Baptist's attitude was admirable and his motives were pure. Jesus First was the motto of his life. And of his life Jesus said, "Among those born of women there has not arisen anyone greater than John the Baptist" (Matt. 11:11). He was a prince of men because he had the Prince of Peace in his heart and in his life. And that is what it will take for us to get our personal priorities in order: the Prince of Peace, dwelling in our hearts and in our lives.

Define your character. When we have developed a proper set of personal priorities in our lives, they will demand that we define our character. It has been well said that life is like a grindstone, and whether it grinds a man down or polishes him depends on the stuff he is made of.

That "stuff" is what makes up character. It is what God knows we are, not what our family, our pastor, our coworkers think we are. It is what we are in the dark, unseen places of our lives. It is exhibited in what we read, what we watch on television, the places we frequent, what strikes us as funny. It is defined by what we carry home from the office in our briefcases, what type movies we check out at the video store, and whether or not we would drive off assuming no accountability after a "minor" fender bender in a deserted parking garage.

Someone once said, "The measure of a man's real character is what he would do if he knew he would never be found out." Character is more than charm or manners. Character is that essence of ourselves that needs no epitaph. Character beats the hearse back from the graveyard.[4]

Daniel: An Example of Personal Priorities

Booker T. Washington is reported to have said, "There is no power on earth that can neutralize the influence of a high, pure, simple, and useful life."[5] A beautiful example of this is found in the life of Daniel in the Old Testament. High, pure, simple, and useful, his life gives every Christian an example of what pleases God in the area of personal priorities.

Daniel stood firm in the principles of faithfulness and commitment to Almighty God. The Bible points out Daniel's outstanding physical appearance, as well as his gifts of knowledge, wisdom, leadership, and dream interpretation. Torn from his home as a boy, he was one of the ones being hustled, hurried, and pushed down that long dusty path from Judah to the empire of Babylon when the people of God were taken into captivity by Nebuchadnezzar's armies in 605 B.C. In this hostile environment, Daniel, his name meaning "God is Judge," stood firm in his faith convictions, assured that God, not man, was in control of his destiny.

How does faith survive a thousand miles from home and church and family? How does faith survive when there are hard, unpopular choices to make? How does faith survive when you are sick of heart, mind, and body, and there is no one there to lean on? How does faith survive when your bright future crashes down around you and you cannot put the pieces of the broken dreams back together?

Faith survives naturally when we allow our personal priorities to be shaped by God's will. Faith is molded and cultivated in the muddy trenches and deep valleys of life. Faith develops in the School of God's Control and is demonstrated when we are able to exhibit self-control. Faith is waiting without whining. Faith is yielding life without reservation. It is hope eternal in the God we have seen only with our hearts, and it is putting our complete trust in Him. Faith is calling God, Lord, and fleshing it out by giving Him control.

That is what Daniel did. He made a conscious decision to maintain his walk with God by giving Him control in the area of his personal priorities. Even though he was just a youth who had no mother or father looking over his shoulder; even though a change of lifestyle would have pleased his captors and secured his status in the Babylonian empire; even though the pleasures of Babylon might have looked tempting to this Hebrew boy; the Word of God says he did not succumb to temptation, nor did he set his course away from God. Let's examine Daniel's priorities.

Priority 1: He Would Not Compromise His Beliefs

Even though he found himself a slave in a foreign country, stripped of his native language, his customs, even his religion, no one could strip him of his God. And with passion he "made up his mind" that in whatever he did, whatever he said, he would serve God and Him alone.

He wouldn't compromise his beliefs by defiling his body. That is why he could not eat the king's appointed daily ration of food or drink the wine. It would have defiled him before God. So he graciously asked permission to change the menu from steak to beans—and permission was granted (Dan. 1:8).

He would not compromise his beliefs by defiling his mind. That is why when a pagan education was forced upon him in a godless school system, he politely listened and then depended on God, who gave him "knowledge and intelligence in every branch of literature and wisdom; Daniel even understood all kinds of visions and dreams" (Dan. 1:17).

He would not compromise his beliefs by defiling his spirit. "Then this Daniel began distinguishing himself [among his coworkers] . . . because he possessed an extraordinary spirit." That is why when faced with the possibility of being a meal for hungry lions, Daniel still chose to worship the Maker of the universe rather than the ruler of this world. He continued to pray, realizing in his spirit that God was a higher authority than any king, and his allegiance, no matter what the consequences, belonged to God.

The story is told of a preacher, who, anxious to be strong in his preaching yet not offensive, said to his confused congregation: "If you do not repent, as it were; and be converted, in a measure; you will go to hell, to a certain extent." While stumbling back and forth, trying to please both God and man, this fellow discovered he had pleased neither.

To be an effective witness, the Christian must make up his mind about some things just as Daniel did. It is very important to know which issues in life demand a firm doctrinal stand and which issues can be negotiated. Daniel did not allow anything to defile his relationship with God and neither should we.

Priority 2: He Always Deliberated and Prayed Before Acting

Nebuchadnezzar, ruler of Babylon, had dreamed a perplexing dream but could not remember its contents. In his frustration he called for his magicians, conjurers, sorcerers, and enchanters—all his wise men and priests—not only to interpret the dream, but also reveal its contents. When they could not meet his unrealistic expectations, he threatened to kill them all.

When news of the impending execution reached the ears of Daniel, the Bible says he handled the matter with "discretion and discernment" (Dan. 2:14), requesting "of the king that he would give him time, in order that he might declare the interpretation" (2:16).

He never participated in evil. On several occasions the Chaldeans, who were the wise men of Babylon, were called before the king to give him counsel; yet, Daniel, even though he was numbered among them, was never with them (2:13).

That is because they were self-seeking, manipulating shysters, and Daniel wanted no part of their evil deeds. Because of that he fell victim to many of their diabolic plots (6:4).

He never panicked under pressure. With the threat of death hanging over his head, Daniel set out quietly to solve the mystery of the king's dream. He gathered a coalition of his trusted, godly friends together and informed them of the situation (2:17). However, he did not ask them for advice on the matter. There was no futile speculative discussion among them on what the nature of the dream might have been. They all knew their source of wise counsel was not their collective intelligence, but God alone.

Victor Hugo once said, "Have courage for the great sorrows of life and patience for the small ones; and when you have laboriously accomplished your daily tasks, go to sleep in peace. God is awake!" [6] Daniel knew that, and therefore he did not whine nor did he waste precious energy worrying. He simply placed his confidence in God.

He consistently prayed for guidance. With a possible crisis facing him, Daniel and his friends looked beyond themselves and "requested compassion from the God of heaven concerning this mystery" (2:18). There is no real information given in the text that reveals the specific amount of time they spent praying. It would seem that they simply prayed, and then without fanfare God answered their prayer by revealing the dream to Daniel in a "night vision" (2:19).

He consistently praised God for His provision. When the answer came and the dream was revealed, he did not immediately race off to King Nebuchadnezzar's chamber. First, Daniel, knowing his source of provision, "blessed the God of heaven" (2:19). And what a glorious blessing it was:

> Let the name of God be blessed forever and ever, for wisdom and power belong to Him.

> And it is He who changes the times and the epochs; He removes kings and establishes kings; He gives wisdom to wise men, and knowledge to men of understanding.
>
> It is He who reveals the profound and hidden things; He knows what is in the darkness, and the light dwells with Him.
>
> To Thee, O God of my fathers, I give thanks and praise, for Thou hast given me wisdom and power; even now Thou hast made known to me what we requested of Thee, for Thou hast made known to us the king's matter.
>
> — Daniel 2:20–23

Tony Campolo tells the story of a little girl who carried a big puff of cotton candy. He looked at her and said, "How can a little girl like you eat so much cotton candy?" "Well, you see," she said, "I am bigger on the inside than on the outside." That is a good definition of the character developed in Daniel's life. He was bigger on the inside than on the outside.

How about you? When office gossip oozes from one desk to another, do you take up a weapon and participate in character assassination? Are you apt to panic when things go wrong on the job and you are placed in a precarious position with the boss? Or is it your habit to turn every crisis over to God in prayer, trusting Him and allowing Him time to work things out His way? And when the blessings come, the crisis is past, do you stop to praise Him for His faithfulness? You do if you're bigger on the inside than on the outside.

Priority 3: He Glorified God and Elevated Others

It is told that on one occasion a Christian brother of St. Francis of Assisi began to yell at him in frustration, saying, "Why thee, why thee? Everybody follows thee, everyone yearns to see thee, hear thee, obey thee, and yet, thou are neither handsome, nor educated, nor of highborn family. Why then should it be thee whom the world prefers to follow?"

Upon hearing those words Francis bowed his head in prayer, praising and blessing God with unusual fervor. Then he addressed his troubled brother. "God chose me because He could find none more worthless, and He wished to confound the nobility and grandeur, the strength, the beauty and the learning of this world."[7]

Like St. Francis, Daniel was not in the business of elevating Daniel. He was very much a background person, but a leader nevertheless. He did not want people to obey or acclaim him. Until times of crisis most people in Babylon rarely knew he existed. He talked little, did his work well, and proved to be a splendid example for others to follow.

He never took credit for what God alone had done. Daniel had a high regard for God and His eternality, as well as an awareness of his own mortality.

In the last century an American tourist paid a visit to a renowned Polish rabbi, Hofetz Chaim. The American was astonished when he saw that the rabbi's house was no more than a simple room, a few books, a table and a bench.

"Where is your furniture?" blurted the tourist.

"Where is yours?" replied the rabbi.

"Mine?" responded the puzzled tourist. "I'm just a visitor here, only passing through."

"So am I," said the rabbi.

Daniel never accepted the glory for what God did in his life because he knew he was just a powerless visitor here, only passing through. He knew he was living on borrowed time, breathing borrowed air, eating food borrowed from the hand of his generous God. When Nebuchadnezzar asked Daniel, "Are you able to make known to me the dream which I have seen and its interpretation?" (2:26), Daniel hastily replied, "As for the mystery about which the king has inquired, neither wise men, conjurers, magicians, nor diviners are able to declare it to the king. However, there is a God in heaven who reveals mysteries" (2:27–28). And Nebuchadnezzar was about to have a firsthand encounter with Him.

He always depended on God for his promotions. There was no consuming ambition in Daniel's life. Wherever he found himself, whoever might be the king, his only ambition was to serve God and present an accurate portrayal of Him to his fellow laborers. Because of his commitment to God and his willingness to follow God's plan for his life, "the king promoted Daniel and gave him many great gifts, and he made him ruler over the whole province of Babylon" (2:48).

A. W. Tozer wrote, "I believe it might be accepted as a fairly reliable rule of thumb that the man who is ambitious to lead is disqualified as a leader."[8]

He never excluded those who served with him. Daniel knew he had not labored alone. He remembered that other men had prayed with him through the night for God to reveal the king's mysterious dream. When Daniel was promoted, he recognized his valuable colaborers, and "Daniel made request of the king and he appointed Shadrach, Meshach and Abed-nego over the administration of the province of Babylon" (2:49). Daniel did not rise to prominence in Babylon on the backs of his friends, but beside them.

The Christian with character, the one who pleases God in the area of personal priorities, will never take credit for what he is not responsible for doing. He will not be motivated by pride, elevating himself at the expense of others. She will depend on God to be her sponsor as well as her benefactor. And she will move beyond petty rivalries and feuds, freeing herself to attempt the impossible: incorporating God into the lives of the people around her.

Daniel's list of personal priorities acted as a road map throughout his life, keeping him on track and headed in the right direction. Unlike the fictitious Alice, who was content to wander aimlessly, Daniel had both a destination for his life and a plan to reach that destination. By establishing and maintaining personal priorities he was able to sift through the material debris of life and unearth its priceless treasures.

I remember the morning when my telephone rang and I received the message that my teenage daughter had been involved in a serious car accident. She and four other girls were on their way to a high school choral competition in a nearby city in North Carolina when a large truck hit them from behind, totaling the brand new car I had just purchased for her.

I was not concerned about that twisted hunk of metal she had been driving. My prayers were for my daughter and those dear ones traveling with her. When I was able to get to her, I threw my arms around her and we both wept—she, because she thought she had destroyed the family treasure; I, because I knew that I held the family treasure in my arms.

If there is nothing in your life that serves as a directional cornerstone, today is the day you must begin to establish a list of personal priorities. To do that you must study the Word of God, examining the lives of the people chronicled within its pages and discover what their priorities were. Explore the teachings of Jesus and pattern your priorities after His. Look at the lives of those who form the pillars of your church. What is it about their lives that keeps them on track? Then incorporate those priorities into your own life by determining in your heart that—regardless of circumstances or personalities—you are resolved to stay on the pathway that leads to God.

FIVE

Building a Magnificent Marriage

Let every husband stay a true lover,
And every wife remain a sweetheart too.[1]

After twenty years of marriage counseling, I have discovered the primary root of all problems in the home is the inability to communicate properly. Couples who do not communicate verbally, emotionally, or physically lose touch with one another's dreams and aspirations. They grow apart rather than grow together. Bitterness develops as they increasingly misunderstand each other's motives and aspirations. When such a marriage dissolves because of infidelity, we often hear the baffled and betrayed partner say, "I didn't know anything was wrong."

That is precisely what happened to Mark and Tracy (not their real names). They moved to town with good jobs and brilliant futures. They found great satisfaction in the promotions, the paychecks, the admiring looks of coworkers, and the positive affirmation of superiors.

Gradually, Mark began to receive more positive affirmation from his job than his marriage. He spent more and more time at the office, submerging himself in the mountain of material that always seemed to cover his desk. He discovered that his professional accomplishments played an important part in how he felt about himself—not to mention the bottom line of his salary.

Tracy, on the other hand, came home night after night to an empty house. Feeling rejected and vulnerable, she finally succumbed to the admiring glances and suggestive compliments of her boss. She was lonely and he had a listening ear, plus plenty of time to make her feel special. She also began to work late, but not alone. Since Mark was so busy, she spent many intimate evenings dining alone with her boss. A flirtation led to a kiss, and soon Tracy, who described herself as a faithful church member and committed Christian, found herself involved in an affair.

Of course, Mark found out about it. Both were devastated. Fortunately, they sought out good Christian counseling that allowed them to step back, reevaluate the direction their lives had taken, and make the necessary adjustments to save their marriage. However, I am afraid they are the exception, not the rule.

In the Bible, we find the same scenario—real couples who were obliged to deal with real-life problems. Adam and Eve were forced to relocate, file for the equivalent of bankruptcy, and live a reduced lifestyle—all because of lack of communication. Abraham and Sarah, because of a childless relationship, opted for surrogate mothering and spent the rest of their lives wishing they had discussed its ramifications more thoroughly. And what about David and Michal, who spent most of their married life separated and bitter, with no communication at all? The Bible is replete with such case studies of couples with communication problems—but it also includes God's genuine solutions to "bigger-than-life" marital problems.

The Core of the Problem: Communication

The core of the couple-communication problem begins in the first chapter of the book of Genesis where God, "created man in His own image, in the image of God He created him; male and female He created them" (Gen. 1:27). Herein lies our dilemma: the pinnacle of God's creation—one man and one woman—who physically looked different, acted out different roles, reacted differently to the same stimuli, and communicated in different ways—did not know what to make of each other.

Review the events in chapter 3 where Eve and then Adam disobeyed God concerning His admonition not to eat the forbidden fruit of the tree of knowledge of good and evil. First, we see the serpent approaching Eve and initiating a long dialogue in an attempt to convince her of two ideas: (1) that God had been less than honest when He predicted that death was the result of disobedience, and (2) that the fruit was desirable as well as beneficial since it would produce, even in mere humans, the godlike characteristic of wisdom.

Upon close examination of the chapter, it is notable that it took the serpent six verses and considerable dialogue to talk Eve into eating the fruit. Yet, in verse 6 we read the words matter-of-factly, "and she gave also to her husband with her, and he ate."

Is the point I am trying to make here that Adam was more easily duped by the crafty serpent than his mate? No! The implication is that the serpent observed the unique differences built into the male and the female and then emphasized those differences to lead Adam and Eve away from God, first individually, then corporately.

Look at his tactics. He isolated Eve and appealed to her need for conversation, affirmation, and knowledge. He spent quality time with her, engaging in dialogue, listening to her question, replying with tenderness, "Don't worry, you surely shall not die!" (v. 4). He also gave validity to her worth as an individual when he encouraged her to be all she could be. "In the day you eat from it your eyes will be opened, and you will be like God, knowing good and evil." (v. 5). He created a deceptive atmosphere where Eve's greatest needs—love and security—seemed to be met. Then, when he won her trust and friendship, he stood back and watched as "she took from its [the tree's] fruit and ate" (v. 6).

And what battle plan did the serpent use that caused Adam to disobey God? Notice that Satan knew better than to speak directly to the man, knowing full well that Adam would remember the words God had spoken specifically to him a few verses earlier, saying, "And the LORD God commanded the man, saying, 'From any tree of the garden you may eat freely; but from the tree of the knowledge of good and evil you shall not eat, for in the day that you eat from it you shall surely die'" (Gen. 2:16–17). This admonition from the Creator came solely to Adam, before Eve was ever created. It is evident from Scripture that she did indeed know the story, but at best her information was secondhand. Adam, however, knew the facts because they had been passed from God directly to him.

That is why Satan knew he could never be persuasive enough to convince Adam that God had misrepresented the facts. Nor would he have been able to use flattering words and false promises to twist Adam's head and distort his thinking. Adam fully knew who God was; there could never have been any confusion about that. No, it was not the serpent who skipped into Adam's presence holding a half-eaten piece of forbidden fruit. It was his young, beautiful, seemingly innocent wife who, intoxicated by her own newfound wisdom, handed her deadly treasure to her husband, anticipating a positive reaction from him.

Adam, being a man, deeply needed his wife's acceptance, her appreciation, and her approval. He must have looked at her, still so alive and vivacious in spite of God's warning. Then, even though he knew better, he threw all caution to the wind, reached out, and took the fruit from the hand of his beloved, trusted companion. With one bite, he realized he had made a horrible, life-changing mistake.

Men and women have an inherent, rebellious bent that inevitably leads them away from God and holy living. That is apparent throughout Scripture as we read account after account of individuals who struggled with doing what is right by God's standards as opposed to doing what is wrong. The apostle Paul wrote, "For I know that nothing good dwells in me, that is, in my flesh; for the wishing is present in me, but the doing of the good is not. For the good that I wish, I do not do; but I practice the very evil that I do not wish" (Rom. 7:18–19). This has dramatic implications concerning marriage.

We have established the fact that even in the marriage "made in heaven"—Adam and Eve's—there are continual struggles for control, dominance, position, and even power between two people who love each other. These struggles, planned or coincidental, eventually cause marital battle fatigue and sometimes lead to the termination of what started out as a beautiful relationship. This was never God's intention when He established the glorious institution of marriage.

Operating Within Your Comfort Zone

Look at man's position in life. Man was created to rule and subdue the marvelous world that God had created: "Then the Lord God took the man and put him into the garden of Eden to cultivate it and keep it" (Gen. 2:15). He was to act as caretaker and administrator over God's good earth. This position earned him the respect of his wife and satisfied one of his greatest needs.

Woman, on the other hand, was fashioned from man for man. She was to act as his companion, as his completer. Because of her existence, man would never again be alone: "Then the LORD God said, 'It is not good for the man to be alone: I will make him a helper suitable for him'" (Gen 2:18). This worthy position in God's creation earned Eve the love of her husband, as well as the security she so desperately desired.

Because of man's God-given nature as a ruler and subduer, his desire is usually to oversee the domains of his world. Therefore, his comfort zone encompasses the world outside the home. He may move freely in and out of the arena of business and finances. Or perhaps he plows his fields and plants his crops; nevertheless, he is comfortable with his role as provider.

Even though many women capably function in the capacity of provider, that was not God's original plan. And if given a choice, many competent, thoughtful women willingly choose to make their dominion their home. There they function with great personal satisfaction as companions and completers to husbands, as well as caregivers in their homes with their children.

The marriage of two people is a relationship that is permanent, pertinent, and proper. It began when God meticulously carved woman out of man's side, symbolizing the fact that one is a vital part of the other, drawing life, as it were, from one another. Biblically, the relationship is a physical and spiritual contract, broken only by the death of one of the partners. It is ordained and established by God Himself for the purpose of oneness and openness and procreation. In a spirit of cooperation a man and a woman can stand side by side and face the difficulties of life, and with the help of God, they can overcome.

When the space shuttle *Challenger* lifted into the sky and exploded seventy-three seconds into its flight in 1986, the world was shocked and horrified. The videotape of that terrible moment shows a deep blue sky marred by twisted trails of smoke and large chunks of metal plummeting toward the ocean. And we know, as we recall the grim specter of the explosion, that among the falling pieces were the bodies of some of America's finest men and women.

The investigations into the cause of the tragedy pointed out some serious shortfalls in human judgment and materials management. One prominent publication proposed that the ultimate cause of the space shuttle disaster was pride. It reported that a group of top managers failed to listen carefully to the warning of subordinates who were concerned about the operational reliability of certain parts of the booster rocket under conditions of abnormal stress, such as those present on the day of the launch. Even though encouraged to change the launch schedule, the people in charge were confident that they should go forward. They were wrong.

Pride and Stress: A Dangerous Duo in Marriage

As in the case of the *Challenger,* many problems in marriage begin with pride and stress. Couples often naively think they will be able to handle anything that comes their way. Yet, according to the Bible, "Pride goes before destruction" (Prov. 16:18) in any relationship. We live in a stress-filled atmosphere and for the most part, we are born to be self-serving and proud individuals, a dangerous duo in marriage.

No marriage is immune to failure. If we need any proof of that, just look at the number of Christian leaders in prominent churches all over America who have floundered in the area of marriage. However, do not despair. God has a plan to reduce the stress and pride that leads to marital battle fatigue and to replace them with Christlike humility that leads to servanthood.

How can we overcome battle fatigue in our marriages? We must be willing to place self on the back burner and discover the major needs of our spouse. Then, equipped with that knowledge we must determine that we will allow God to meet those needs through us.

Seven Needs in Marriage

Each marriage partner has areas of basic need and every area has to do with communication, either verbal, emotional, or physical. Addressing each area is critical if we are to lay the foundation and framework for a successful marriage. All secondary needs are tied up in these primary areas, making them crucial to harmonious coexistence with the opposite sex within the bonds of marriage.

A Relationship with God vs. Spiritual Emptiness

There is an interesting story about the CEO of a Fortune 500 corporation who was so impressed by a book entitled *Men and Women of God* that he called a downtown Chicago bookstore and ordered 350 copies of it to give to all the supervisors in his company. The bookstore sent back a message by computer that read: "We cannot find 350 Men and Women of God in Chicago. Try Los Angeles."

Nothing will drive our marriages toward disaster, and individuals toward battle fatigue, faster than spiritual emptiness. Dealing with all the dynamics of marriage (and the relationships that spring from that union) can be a totally draining experience for the couple who faces that challenge alone. When our emotional, psychological, and even physical strength is depleted, little irritations become significant, and major crises become intolerable. At that point marriages begin to slowly dissolve as the battles of life relentlessly inflict wounds, building scar tissue on hearts that once beat with hopes and dreams and love.

If our marriages are to be all we want them to be, we need help. The most critical area of need for both spouses is a dynamic, personal relationship with God. You will never have a marriage made in heaven unless you have heaven's help with your marriage. Psalm 127:1 says, "Unless the Lord builds the house, they labor in vain who build it." A marriage foundation built on anything besides the Cornerstone, Jesus Christ, will deteriorate from without and within and eventually crumble and fall. The apostle Paul admonished, "Do not be bound together with unbelievers . . . what has a believer in common with an unbeliever?" (2 Cor. 6:14–15).

The ideal marriage relationship takes on the shape of an equilateral triangle. The apex is symbolized by God, with the two equal sides representing the individual marriage partners. The base of the triangle represents Jesus Christ. The analogy infers that both partners, grounded in faith in Jesus Christ, are continually moving upward toward a loving relationship with God. The perfect picture then is two individuals, moving closer to one another in the marriage relationship, while also ascending upward toward God and spiritual maturity.

If this is not the case in your marriage, you are probably frustrated and perplexed, fearing that this picture may never represent your home. Do not be discouraged! It is not your job to change your mate, but God's. It is your job to remain faithful in prayer for that mate. When God straightens out His vertical relationship with your mate, the horizonal relationship with you will fall beautifully into place.

Active Love vs. Stagnant Apathy

Another critical area of need in marriage is genuine love. Love means more than romance, family loyalty, or friendship. In a marriage, love must eventually transcend the physical and move toward the spiritual or it is categorized merely as lust.

Three types of love are routinely spoken of in the Bible, and all three are important for a healthy marriage. The first is *eros*, a possessing kind of love; a passionate, all-absorbing love that requires pleasure if it is to continue to exist. Closely akin to our English word *erotic*, it does have a valuable place in a Christian marriage. *Eros* has the ability to transform a boring, humdrum marriage into a glorious fireworks display.

The second type of love that appears in the New Testament is *phileo*. While *eros* creates lovers, *phileo* has the capacity to foster friendships. Those who have *phileo* love share experiences, communicate intimacies, and enjoy one another's companionship. Yet, even with all its benefits, this type of love always expects a response from the one being loved. "As long as you love me, I'll love you back. As long as you cherish me, I'll cherish you. As long as you share with me, I'll share with you," are common attitudes expressed by *phileo* love. In a marriage it is important to express *phileo* love in order to form that bond of intimate friendship so necessary for a healthy relationship between two people.

The third and most lasting kind of love is *agape*, a totally selfless love. It has the capacity to give and continue giving without expecting anything in return. *Agape* love serves the recipient of its affection. It is the same kind of love exhibited by Jesus Christ when He willingly died on the cross so that we might be reconciled to God. Both *eros* and *phileo* love eventually end when, after an extended period of time, there is no response. But *agape* love can survive anything since it is not based on emotion, but is a deliberate choice of the will. *Agape* love has its source in God; therefore, it loves, no matter what happens. There are times in every marriage when the loving is based on choice, not on feelings alone. It is during these hard, uncertain times that marriages are held together by tough, uncompromising, thoroughly committed *agape* love.

The art of being in love and maintaining a love relationship is no small feat. A successful relationship takes hard work. Willard F. Harley Jr., in his book *His Needs, Her Needs*, made a profound statement concerning marriage. He said, "Marriage is not a simple social institution that everyone eventually enters into because he or she 'falls in love and lives happily ever after.' As long as we fail to see marriage as a complex relationship that requires special training and abilities to meet the needs of a member of the opposite sex, we will continue to see a discouraging and devastating divorce rate."[2]

Time to Talk vs. Time to Listen

Another key element in expressing our love involves developing the fine art of communication. People who love one another take time to listen to one another.

It happened at their golden wedding anniversary party. The husband was touched by the event and wanted to tell his wife just how much he cared for her. She was extremely deaf, however, and often misunderstood what he said. With the whole family and many friends gathered around, he praised her: "My dear wife, after fifty years I've found you tried and true!"

Everyone smiled in admiration. But unable to hear, his wife said, "Eh?"

He repeated louder, "AFTER FIFTY YEARS I'VE FOUND YOU TRIED AND TRUE!"

With this his wife made some undistinguishable guttural sounds and shot back, "Well, let me tell you something— after fifty years I'm tired of you, too!"

As with this dear couple, the problem in marriage is often not inability to listen, but the incapacity to hear exactly what was actually said. Concerning the obvious communication problem between the sexes, one husband has aptly said to his wife, "I know you believe you understand what you think I said, but I'm not sure you realize that what you heard is not what I meant." Confused? So was his wife.

While both women and men engage in prolific conversation during their courtship, a major shutdown of dialogue seems to gradually take place soon after marriage. I have observed married couples walk into a nice restaurant, obviously anticipating a lovely evening together—and the only words spoken after they were seated were those shared with the waitress as she took their orders.

There is an interesting theory about why couples "terminate talking." Some marriage counselors contend that men and women speak different languages and therefore cannot easily understand one another.

Oscar Wilde once wittingly said, "Women are to be loved, not understood." While I do not believe that it is impossible to understand women, it is true that men are more literal while women speak figuratively. Men process thoughts inwardly, while it is important for a woman to process information verbally, often to another significant person in her life. Women use superlatives and generalizations in talking. Men want just "the facts, ma'am."

If communication is so important, what must couples do to begin talking to one another again? I have a simple proposal that will necessitate a compound response. Spouses must take time to sit across from one another, look each other in the eye, sincerely and honestly share themselves verbally—and never, never, never look at their watches.

For the sake of your marriage, talk to your mate. Value and respect your spouse as a trustworthy, intelligent listener, capable of interacting with you on your level. Build self-esteem in your mate by confiding in him or her your personal victories as well as defeats. Share your life and your time; it's the most precious gift you can give to the one you love.

Here are a few hints that may help keep the pizazz in your marriage:

> Make the routine unforgettable. Little things mean a lot in a marriage. Hugs and kisses are important at every age and every stage.

- Create unique moments. Make sure there is at least one every week. Flowers or a thoughtful card tend to make any moment special.
- Contribute to future memories. Make long-term plans to be together. Discuss your dreams. Set attainable goals. Work together to accomplish them.
- Reminisce about the past. Talk about how far God has brought you together. Discuss the struggles as well as the times of rejoicing. Build that bond of oneness that makes life without each other seem unnatural.
- Express your feelings openly. Say, "I love you!" Say it! Write it! Live it!

Timeless Trust vs. Devastating Doubt

Couples need to be able to trust one another. A marriage built on trust involves two important things: honesty and cooperation. Without both honesty and cooperation, a marriage will not survive. A trust problem often occurs when one or both partners refuses, or is afraid, to open up and reveal his or her true feelings. Yet, without complete honesty between married couples, the relationship lacks integrity as well as exhibits a breach in confidence between partners.

It is never appropriate for couples to lie, misrepresent, or hide the truth from one another. The truth builds emotional security in the home, it enables couples to communicate as well as negotiate with one another, and it makes life more predictable and dependable. Trust comes, not as a result of one single truth, but through numerous experiences when both husband and wife are able, in complete honesty and willing cooperation, to prove themselves trustworthy. To build a sense of trust in a marriage relationship it is important to:

- Touch each other, just for the sake of touching. A gentle hand on the shoulder communicates security and stability in any situation. It says, "I am here. You are not alone. With me you are safe."

> Develop open lines of communication where "honesty really is the best policy." Foster an atmosphere where conversation is welcome and nonjudgmental. Be careful not to concentrate too much on past grievances. Be forgiving, and, as much as possible forgetting.

> Be sensitive to your mate's physical, psychological, emotional, social, and spiritual needs and work to meet those needs as best you can. Ways to meet these needs will become more evident as you spend quality time getting acquainted with your mate.

> Work hard at developing a relationship based on mutual acceptance and respect. Remember, no one is perfect. Don't be tempted to turn attempts at conversation into lecture periods geared toward changing your mate's attitude or actions. If that happens to be the purpose of the discussion, make it known at the beginning of the discussion to keep down confusion.

> Be generous with kisses, hugs, love notes, bouquets, and "I love yous." As always, communicate your love.

Reasonable Respect vs. Contrived Contempt

Every person needs someone to say, "I value you. I value your opinion. You have great worth as a human being." Approval is so important to an individual's self-image that he or she will go to drastic means to satisfy that craving, sometimes seeking it outside the marriage. Men especially need their wives to be proud of their accomplishments. In ancient times when a man came home from the hunt, there was a celebration where his exploits, his acts of bravery, and his skill and cunning in the hunt were all repeated around the campfire, over and over again. Not so today. In our society, when a man comes home from the rigors of the day, more often than not, he has nothing tangible to show for his effort. In this era of modern technology even the monthly check may have already been directly deposited in his bank account or, worse, already spent before he brings it home. Consequently, there is usually no recognition for his being a good provider and no gratification for being a hero to his family, unless he hears it from his partner.

A word of caution: Marriage partners must learn to appreciate and respect one another for what they already are, not for what they have the potential to become if prodded. Destructive criticism—the phrase itself almost hisses—puts partners on the defensive and stifles creativity. But admiration and genuine respect motivate.

In Westport, Connecticut, a bride and groom exchanged vows—then pushes and finally shoves. They were fighting over the custom of cramming the wedding cake into the face of one's beloved. The newlyweds were arrested after their wedding reception on charges of disturbing the peace. When questioned, the bride said her new husband fed her the cake too roughly. Fighting resulted when she responded in kind, and someone called the police.

Handling Conflict vs. Volatile Explosions

It's inevitable! Eventually something will come up that has the potential to explode into an argument. All couples experience differences and disagreements, yet successful couples seem to have developed compensating styles for handling conflict within marriage. Psychologist John Gottman, author of the book *What Predicts Divorce*, defines three basic types of stable marriages and their conflict management techniques.

Marriage 1 is composed of "volatile couples" who fight a lot but also laugh a lot. These couples seem to thrive on combat. However, their arguing does not include caustic criticism or sarcastic put-downs. To do so might cause violent behavior between the partners.

Marriage 2 is composed of "validating couples" who temper their emotional outbursts and have a strong sense of "we-ness." These couples have always been regarded by researchers as having the best chance for marital "bliss" and longevity.

Marriage 3 is composed of "conflict-avoidant couples" who sweep most differences under the rug. These couples are usually more traditional and embrace traditional, stereotypical gender roles.[3]

In the past, researchers did not give either volatile couples or conflict-avoidant couples much credit for successful conflict management. However, newer research suggests that the relationships that are most likely to end in divorce may not be those in which spouses argue passionately or often. Nor is a marriage doomed when couples agree to avoid conflict by suppressing their hostile feelings toward one another.

Gottman, as well as several other respected researchers, has discovered four chronic behaviors that cause a marriage to dissolve. They are criticism, contempt, defensiveness, and withdrawal.[4] Here is the scenario:

The wife realizes her needs are not being met and attempts to compensate or turn a particular situation around by using criticism. When criticism does not implement the desired response from her husband, she often feels contempt toward him. Her husband, on the other hand, combats his wife's offensive onslaught by immediately going on the defensive and withdrawing to a safe place out of the range of fire. On the one hand, we have a wife engaged in all-out war to prove her point or win her battle, while we see her mate engaged in a cold war, silent and seemingly unaffected by her passionate outbursts. You can see how this could become a vicious cycle with both partners miserable.

We must do something about the battle zone in our home. The story goes like this: A woman consulted a medium, who was able to put her in touch with her departed husband.

"Adam," said the woman, "are you happy now?"

"I am very happy," responded the spirit of Adam.

"Are you happier than you were on earth with me?"

"Yes, I am much happier than I was on earth with you."

"Tell me, Adam," asked the woman. "What's it like in heaven?"

"Heaven!" bellowed Adam. "I'm not in heaven!"

A marriage need not deteriorate to the point where one or both partners have to leave it to find happiness. While conflict is inevitable—especially in the sensitive areas of communication, sex, and money—without the added ingredients of contempt and defensiveness, it is manageable.

Disagreement and anger can turn ugly and be very harmful to a marriage if shared communication is not a priority for both spouses. Here are some suggestions that might help you and your mate ward off unnecessary conflict.

- Set up some ground rules for making conflict creative, not caustic. Agree to disagree about issues, not personalities. Don't get sidetracked; stick to the main issue. And *never* vilify your mate's family while arguing.
- Communicate grievances in a quiet manner that does not terrorize or tear down your mate. Convey an atmosphere of safety and love where feelings are validated and hurts can be expressed without intimidation.
- Learn techniques that help avoid marital conflict. If you know leaving the lid up on the toilet in the middle of the night has caused her anxiety in the past, do not do it anymore.
- Be honest and open about your feelings, but do not express them in a way that could be personally insulting and offensive to your mate.
- Always leave the door open for negotiating that leads to reconciliation. Keep in mind that neither you nor your

mate is perfect, and anger is an expression of that imperfection. It is possible to "be angry and sin not" (Eph. 4:26) if anger is handled in a mature fashion.

Do not wait until bitterness and resentment have robbed you of the joys of your marriage before you do something about the battle zone in your home. Respect is a natural outpouring when both partners successfully strive to meet one another's basic needs. The apostle Paul encouraged mutual respect: "Nevertheless let each individual among you also love his own wife even as himself; and let the wife see to it that she respect her husband" (Eph. 5:33). The Greek word *phobeo* translated in the text literally means "to be in awe." Few women have trouble respecting, "being in awe," of men who love them as they love themselves. That man considers her needs as important as his own. He can be depended on to support her emotionally, physically, psychologically, and financially. He can be trusted to come home every night. His desire is for his family, and their welfare is important to him. He is interested in what is going on in his wife's life and proves it by spending time with her, conversing, listening, and then responding.

A woman's natural response to a husband such as the one just described is appreciation and respect. She is therefore more open to discovering and meeting his needs. Her level of trust is heightened and she is comfortable with his companionship and sexual advances.

Sexual Fulfillment vs. Insufficient Intimacy

That brings us to the seventh basic need, sexual fulfillment, which will never be accomplished without putting into practice each of the first six previously mentioned areas. You see, unless you are convinced that it was God's intent that "the two become one," your sexual hangups will become a barrier to fulfillment. Without the assurance of love from your partner, along with his or her trust and respect, you will become bitter and alienated, rationalizing that your body is simply an object of gratification for an emotionally uninvolved partner.

It is important to note that men and women enter marriage from opposite ends of the sexual spectrum. He is easily aroused and seemingly always ready. She is more contemplative, seeking emotional attachment, affection, attentiveness, warmth, kindness, tenderness, and sensitivity. Without knowledge of these important differences in the male and female sex drives, and a plan to compensate for the differences, frustration and disappointment—true signs of battle fatigue—are inevitable in the biblical "marriage bed."

Men are bottom-line, fact-oriented people. They have the capacity to meet a situation head-on, size it up, correct the problem, and move on. Not necessarily so with most women. While they too are problem solvers, they tend to be more relational, personable individuals. They meet that same situation encountered by men, but move through it differently because they tend to internalize and personalize every aspect of the situation, taking note of how it directly applies to them.

These particular dynamics, unless compensated for, can cause a rift in sexual fulfillment even between two mutually consenting partners. Because his sexual penchant can be ignited quickly, the male's tremendous appetite says, "Satisfy me at all costs . . . *now!*" While the woman's more fragile sexual desire says, "Romance me, tell me I'm pretty, set a mood . . . then we'll be intimate." Since research indicates that the average married couple spends less than two hours in actual physical lovemaking per week, it would seem logical that the quality of that lovemaking is determined by what goes on during the other 166 hours of the week.

Couples can experience romantic feelings throughout the duration of their lives together if they will practice a few simple rules of etiquette for staying in love—or perhaps falling back into love. It is possible for marriage to become more exciting, not less so, as the years go by.

- Rule 1. Avoid concentrating on your mate's flaws. Stop criticizing and start appreciating.
- Rule 2. Set the right emotional atmosphere by assuring your mate of your love, admiration, and your enthusiasm to be with him/her.
- Rule 3. As life becomes more complicated, make a conscious effort to set aside time for private, intimate moments together when you create a physical atmosphere where romantic love can germinate: dim the lights, light a fire, take a moonlit stroll on the beach, or plan a rendezvous at your favorite restaurant.
- Rule 4. Be creative; avoid boredom in lovemaking. Helen Rowland expressed marital monotony best when she said, "Marriage is the miracle that transforms a kiss from a pleasure into a duty." What an indictment against boredom in marriage. Use your God-given imagination to create pleasurable memories by devising new and exciting emotional and physical experiences with your lover.
- Rule 5. Never use nagging or ridicule against your partner as a tool to get your way in the relationship. Both these tactics close doors to romance and harbor blame, bitterness, and mistrust.
- Rule 6. Always continue to grow together in love. Growing love is living love, thrilling love, vibrant love—at any age.

In marriage, as in all of life, in order to overcome the obstacles and the stresses that everyday living brings with it, couples must grow to love God most, each other more, and self less.

It is told that in the Hawaiian Islands it used to be the custom to give cows as a dowry for brides. If a man wanted to get married he would have to buy his bride by giving her father cows. Three cows were considered to be the price of a valuable young woman. Someone even remembered a bride who had brought five cows, but that was so uncommon that no one could really verify it.

On the big island there was a man who had two daughters. The youngest was a beauty. Some wagered she would bring at least five cows when she married. Her older sister, however, was a different story. Someone had overheard her father saying, "If a man offered me one cow for my homely Mary, I would take it with no questions asked." Knowing how her father and the other villagers felt about her chances for marriage, she stopped hoping for a husband.

One day Johnny Lingo came to the island. He was known to be a rich and wealthy farmer. To everyone's surprise, Johnny asked for Mary's hand in marriage, and surpassing all former dowries, he willingly offered her startled father ten cows. They were married and left for an extended honeymoon.

Time passed and then one day the unsuspecting villagers looked out from their windows and saw Johnny and a strange, but somehow familiar, woman coming back to the village for a visit. All the villagers easily recognized Johnny, but where was Mary, and who was this exquisite lady by his side? She was poised, carried herself with dignity, and was beautiful to behold.

You can imagine their shock when they realized that the homely Mary had transformed into the lovely lady by Johnny's side. Why? Because he had treated her like a ten-cow wife, she had voluntarily become one.

Goethe expressed it this way: "If you treat a man as he is he will stay as he is. If you treat him as if he were what he ought to be and could be, he will become that bigger and better man." In order to escape the dullness and doldrums of life, to make life interesting, give your mate something to live up to, and you will end up with a better mate. This is the key to a magnificent marriage and the cure for marital battle fatigue.

S I X

Prospering in a Profession

We make a living by what we get.
But we make a life by what we give.

Author Unknown

I once heard it said, "The world is composed of takers and givers. The takers may eat better, but the givers sleep better."[1] That was the case when an American pastor visited a newly built church in a small city in the Philippines. During his visit he was taken to the residence of a dear couple who certainly did not appear to be wealthy, yet their home seemed larger and sturdier than others in the city.

When the American pastor admired the home, the wife smiled, motioned toward the house, and replied, "We saved for many years to build this. Each time we got a few pesos ahead, we bought some lumber and stored it in preparation for building. Then we found out that the Presbyterians had decided to build a chapel in the area but had no building materials. So we donated our accumulated lumber to them. Again we began the process of saving up enough boards to build our home, but just when we had enough a Methodist pastor moved into the area and needed our lumber to start a building for his congregation. We were both Methodists, so once again we gave our timbers. A few years later, for the third time, we had enough lumber for a home. 'Let's build it, quick!' we said, 'before the Baptists come!'"[2]

Those generous folks had the capacity not only to build their own lives, but to build Christ into the lives of the people in their city. They labored for years to gain the materials necessary to build a simple home for themselves, but when Christ needed those materials, they were willing to place His will and the wants of others before their own comfort. Their lives were a personification of Matthew 6:19–21, which says, "Do not lay up for yourselves treasures upon earth, where moth and rust destroy, and where thieves break in and steal. But lay up for yourselves treasures in heaven, where neither moth nor rust destroys, and where thieves do not break in or steal; for where your treasure is, there will your heart be also."

Is this verse an indictment against having nice things? No, it is simply an indictment against living and working for the express purpose of accumulating money or commodities while excluding God and others. It is an indictment against making a living while we ignore building a life.

Making a Living or Building a Life?

Most of us are duty bound to make a living. If you fall into that category, let me ask you some questions about your job. Only honest answers please!

Do you like your job? Are you excited about being there? Are you convinced that your being there on a daily basis makes a positive contribution to both your profession and your company? Could the company easily replace you and go on?

The answers to these questions reveal your level of fulfillment in the area of your employment. If you are dissatisfied with your job, that will adversely affect a huge portion of your life since you probably spend the better part of your waking hours there. The Christian lifestyle is designed to free you from the drudgery of a job that could be identified as "prescribed weekday slavery." If practiced authentically, Christianity enables us to enjoy each day of our lives, not just weekends.

A recent survey pinpointed contributing factors influencing human longevity, and the number one indicator for long life was prolonged satisfaction and gratification in the work place. With this information in mind, we should pursue a profession that we find enjoyable. Those just starting out in a career might follow this rule of thumb: Find employment performing tasks that are so enjoyable that you would gladly do them for nothing. That way feelings of gratification and satisfaction will always be balancing factors against improper remuneration and job-related bitterness. For those who feel trapped on the professional treadmill, readjustment of priorities is necessary from simply making a living to building a life.

In his book *Living Abundantly,* Brian Harbour does not relegate the significance of our jobs to the amount of monetary compensation we receive from them. He says, "As Christians, we have a responsibility to do our work in such a way that is pleasing to our Lord. The desire to please Him is the primary motive of Christians in the marketplace."[3] I would take that generalization one step farther by stating that a life pleasing to Him is a life in which He is glorified. Hebrews 13:20–21 substantiates this: "Now the God of peace . . . equip you in every good thing to do His will, working in us that which is pleasing in His sight, through Jesus Christ, to whom be the glory forever and ever. Amen."

Holding down a job must mean more than making a living or that particular job will become a source of battle fatigue in our lives. If we view our jobs as simply avenues to financial security or social prestige, we will become bitter and angry when the raise is delayed or the promotion does not materialize. Unless we see the workplace as a platform from which we can change the world, one person at a time, we will miss the eternal purpose in being there.

One of the keys to happiness and fulfillment on the job is the element of success. The word for *success* in the Bible is usually translated "prosper." It refers to continual professional growth, getting better at job performance, being an eager learner. To prosper also means "pushing forward and broadening horizons." It means having professional dreams and aspirations, not just at the beginning of a career, but throughout its duration.

Success in the truest sense has nothing to do with making money, although money is a well-deserved, tangible reward for a job well done. But financial remuneration alone will not bring fulfillment. Fulfillment comes when a person senses he is making a valuable contribution to a corporate effort. A worker at any level who is fulfilled in his profession will strive harder to do a good job. This brings positive affirmation and sometimes even additional responsibility. The job then becomes an avenue of opportunity to make a real difference, rather than a responsibility to be endured until retirement.

A job becomes what we make of it. What we get out of it often depends on what we are willing to put into it. It has been well said: "One man gets nothing but discord out of a piano; another gets harmony. No one claims the piano is at fault. Life is about the same. The discord is there, and the harmony is there. Study to play it correctly, and it will give forth the beauty; play it falsely, and it will give forth the ugliness. Life is not at fault."[4]

So it is with the job. We must not sell ourselves short by just scratching and clawing to make the house payment and adding to our collection of "stuff." As a Christian we have the ability to add some harmony to this dissonant world when we incorporate Christ into our workday.

What You Do Is Important!

As a child, I remember watching a performance of Leonard Bernstein and the New York Philharmonic. I noticed that in front of Bernstein was an individual who seemed to be doing nothing to contribute to the orchestra's performance. Others were playing instruments, but this particular gentleman simply sat there in his tuxedo, absorbed in the music, turning pages of sheet music at appropriate times. However, as the melody began to gradually get louder, he stirred, picked up an instrument, placed it to his lips and began to play a haunting counter melody. He was not playing the dominant melody but an ancillary one. Nevertheless, without his contribution the symphony would have sounded hollow.

Now, on your job, into which category do you fall? Are you a dominant or a secondary melody person? Both are important. The trumpet may be louder, but the oboe stands out just as vividly simply because of its unique sound quality. There in the workplace and throughout life, God wants to use your life to write a symphony of praise unto Himself.

God has given each of us twenty-four usable hours each day. Within that time frame we allocate periods for sleep, recreation, refueling, and work. Daniel Burnham has said of these precious, nonrenewable hours, "Make no little plans; they have no magic to stir men's blood and probably themselves will not be realized. Make big plans; aim high in hope and work, remembering that a noble, logical diagram once recorded will never die, but long after we are gone will be a living thing, asserting itself with ever-growing insistency."[5]

Three Types of Christians in the Workplace

No Dream, No Plans

There are those folk who do not dream, nor do they make big plans. They never get beyond the present, and they are not motivated to contemplate the impact their job contribution will have on the future. These people have no long-range goals. They are like the college student who I talked to on a local university campus. I asked him what he was going to do, and his dispassionate reply was, "Go eat lunch."

The person in this category is almost perpetually "out to lunch." He does not update his job skills by taking advantage of training opportunities, and he is frightened when a coworker suggests the possibility of a new challenge with redefined areas of responsibility. This person seldom notices opportunities to share his faith in the workplace, rationalizing that church, not the office, is the place where people meet Christ; and the pastor, not the layman, shoulders the burden of witnessing. He is like the little boy who attended summer camp. Upon his return home, his parents asked him if any of the other campers had teased him about being a Christian. "Oh no," was his reply. "They never found out."

Big Dreams, No Action

The second group dreams the big dreams, but they never do anything about implementing those dreams. They always find an excuse for not moving beyond their comfort zone. They are the "suggesters," those who can point out the deficiencies and inconsistencies in the lives of others, but are incapable, or perhaps inept, at pinpointing those same areas in their own lives—or compensating for them. They are content to impress their coworkers with lofty ideas and high-minded proposals, while shrewdly calculating how they will divorce themselves from the extra effort demanded to bring their plans to fruition.

As a young man, President Jimmy Carter graduated from the Naval Academy and served as an officer on a nuclear-powered submarine. However, before he was able to assume that position, he had to have a personal interview with Admiral Hyman Rickover, the man considered to be the father of the nuclear navy. Carter was understandably nervous, knowing how much was at stake and that only the best, most disciplined officers were chosen to serve in this prestigious force.

When he stood before Rickover, it was soon obvious to the young officer that the wise admiral knew more about nearly every subject discussed than did he. Finally Rickover came to the last question on his seemingly never-ending list. "Where did you finish in your class, young man?"

Pleased with his accomplishments and thrilled to finally be presented a question he was sure of, Carter informed the Admiral that he had finished 59th out of a student body numbering 820. Then he waited for a commendation from the old sailor, but it never came.

Jimmy Carter later recounted the incident.

"Did you always do your best?" was the question that broke the uncomfortable silence between the two men.

Carter thought and then cleared his throat. "No, sir, I did not," was his hesitant reply.

Rickover turned his chair around signaling the interview was over and asked, "Why not?"[6]

One day the only question we will have to answer concerning our work is, "Did you always do your best?" not, "Did you have cooperative Christian coworkers?"; not "Was your work space adequate?"; not, "Did you like your boss?" No, the question will be about the dreams God placed in our hearts and minds. Did they just lay there and never take root, buried under tons of good intentions? Or did we do our best to allow God to use us to make a difference in our workplace? Were we like the little girl who fell and skinned her knee? Even though it obviously hurt, she did not cry. When asked how she managed not to cry, she answered, "Oh, I just said to myself, 'Stop that!' and made myself mind me." Make yourself mind you. Whatever God has given you the capacity to dream, with His help, just do it!

Big Dreams, Stunning Results

Some people dream big dreams and then do something to realize those dreams. These folk discerned quickly that God placed them in their particular vocation for a purpose. Through the study of His Word and the activity of prayer, God revealed His purpose in their daily endeavors. They therefore responded by trusting Him to bring about His purpose in their lives, that of moving Christianity from the "secret place" to the "marketplace."

There are many biblical examples of those who accomplished great things for God in the workplace: Solomon built the magnificent temple where thousands of Jews worshiped God. Nehemiah rebuilt the walls of Jerusalem, making it possible for God's people to return and inhabit the land. Esther and Deborah were valiant women who saved their nation from destruction at the hands of the enemies of the Lord. Joseph literally dreamed a dream that, when fleshed out in his life, saved a nation from starvation. And Moses brought Israel out of Egypt and to the doorstep of the promised land. All these people allowed God to use them in the area of their work, and look what great things He accomplished through them!

The person in this third category has come to the realization that true Christianity is about serving God with all his or her heart, soul, mind, and body. This cannot be done exclusively behind the walls of a church. It is a way of life—the Christ way. Because of this radical way of thinking, faith is incorporated—not eliminated—from the workplace. God then becomes the Boss, and life becomes a pulpit expressing His love to all those who cross our path, not obtrusively, but respectfully and unpretentiously. With this perspective on work, we can eagerly anticipate each new day, knowing that God has equipped us, not only to make a living, but to touch lives. Each day is a challenge filled with a mission—full of holy adventure—when your attitude about God results in action in the workplace.

Burned Out and Miserable on the Job?

Are you burned out and miserable in your job? There are several warning signs for those suffering from professional battle fatigue. Have you experienced any of the following symptoms: rapid pulse, frequent illness, insomnia, persistent fatigue, irritability, lack of concentration? If so, perhaps it is because you are a slave.

"A slave," you object with outrage. "I am no slave!"

Well, take a short test and see whether or not you have any slave characteristics. Do you have at least one revolving charge card? Are you making car payments? Do you have a thirty-year mortgage on your home? Do you pay college tuition, utility bills, insurance bills, medical bills, not to mention taxes, taxes, taxes? Do you have the option to quit your job tomorrow, or would that mean financial disaster?

It is true! We are not free. We have forced ourselves into a position that necessitates staying on the job simply because we must make enough money to sustain our lifestyles. Sometimes that means every eligible person in the house is employed while the house itself, the one with the thirty-year mortgage, sits empty. We are thus owned by the system, and that was not God's intention for us when He gave us meaningful labor.

A first-grade student noticed that every night his daddy kept bringing work home from the office. Finally, sick of being deprived of his daddy's company, he said, "Daddy, why don't they put you in a slower group? Then you won't have to work so hard when you get home." Perhaps some of us need to reevaluate our lifestyles and move to another group, one that gives its students time to smell the flowers. After all, if the never-ending pursuit of the better life shortens our lives, is it really better? Many of the professionally fatigued people I have counseled tell me, "I hate my job and I hate those I work for. I am determined to put forth the least amount of effort possible while on the job." Quite frankly, that kind of an attitude in a Christian's life will destroy his witness for Christ in the workplace, as well as Christ's influence in the lives of his coworkers. Instead of using the workplace for what God intended (a fertile garden for planting Christ in the lives of coworkers), it becomes a place where the Christian life is invalidated, discredited, and undercut by the actions of disgruntled believers.

Change Your Attitude: Go the Second Mile

That attitude is 180 degrees removed from Jesus' teaching about what the Christian life is to be. His teachings include turning the other cheek and going the second mile. He encourages Christians to live on a higher plane than those non-Christians around them because their citizenship is in the kingdom of God, where more is expected. George Hodges agrees when he says a real Christian "tries to be the kind of neighbor Christ would be, and the kind of citizen Christ would be, and who asks himself in all the alternatives of his business life, and his social life, and his personal life, 'What would the Master do in this case?' The best Christian is he who most reminds the people with whom he lives of the Lord Jesus Christ. He who never reminds anybody of the Lord Jesus Christ is not a Christian at all."[7]

The second-mile principle can be found in Roman law. Jesus mentioned it in Matthew 5:41 when He said, "And whoever shall force you to go one mile, go with him two." This law gave a soldier in an occupied country the right to require anyone, at any time, to carry his heavy baggage one mile, through any kind of terrain, under any type weather conditions. That mile was 4,848 feet, about 432 feet shorter than our American mile.

Just imagine: a businessman in the marketplace ready to pull off a lucrative deal, a young man on his way to school, or a farmer plowing his field in the spring; and along comes a Roman soldier who throws down his dusty bags, ordering one of them to carry those bags for the required mile.

"Out of the question!" you say. "Inconvenient, inopportune, untimely!" Yes, it was all this and more, but it was the law. And Jesus used this unpopular law to shock everyone around Him when He suggested that believers not only carry the bags the required mile but an extra mile, a second mile, to prove they were kingdom people and that God really did make a difference in their lives.

When we walk the annoying second mile, knowing that act of obedience pleases God, we no longer carry the burden for the uncaring taskmaster, but for God. That gives the unpleasant task an eternal purpose and makes it more palatable. That is the way God wants us to approach the tasks that come with our jobs.

Please do not misunderstand! I am not suggesting that second mile-ism constitutes taking on tasks that are specifically designated for our coworkers. Christ does not condone laziness on the part of any of His children. Picking up another's duties just for the sake of getting the job done faster or "your way," or because that coworker refuses to do his fair share is not second mile-ism—and it will wear us too thin to effectively complete our designated tasks. Certainly, on occasion picking up the load and carrying it for an overburdened coworker is appropriate. However, second mile-ism, while inconvenient, has a greater purpose: glorifying the Father.

If we are Christians, all that we do is to be done for the glory of God. From the most simple to the most complex task, from the mundane to the extraordinary, the attitude and expertise with which we complete each task is a reflection of our heavenly Father in our life and does not go unnoticed by those who labor beside us.

Characteristics of Second-Mile People

Commitment. To commit is to give all that you have and all that you are in trust to God. J. Hudson Taylor said,

> It does not matter where He places me or how. That is rather for Him to consider than for me. For the easiest positions He must give grace; and in the most difficult His grace is sufficient. So, if God places me in great perplexity, must He not give me much guidance? In positions of great difficulty, much grace? In circumstances of great pressure and trial, much strength? As to work, mine was never so plentiful, so responsible, or so difficult; but the weight and strain are all gone. His resources are mine, for He is mine.[8]

Second-mile people do not mind serving in the workplace because they are committed to God. As believers, we do all that we do for Him. Therefore, we should desire to be the best we can be in the workplace, at all times and in the right spirit, in order to please Him. We do this by concentrating on the significance of the job God has placed us in and by thoroughly committing ourselves to completing it. Commitment to excellence comes when we realize the significance of our work in our own lives as well as its benefits in the lives of others.

It is said that during World War II, the United States government ordered thousands of extra parachutes to be used by soldiers fighting overseas. The job of making the parachutes was monotonous, tiresome, and dull. Stretched beyond their capacity, weary workers huddled over sewing machines in dimly lit factories for hours, even days, with little rest. The job could have been intolerable, the work could have become sloppy, had they not been reminded every morning that some of their husbands, their brothers, their sons would be using those chutes, and their very lives depended on them. The knowledge of the significance of their work ensured a high level of commitment in their jobs.[9]

Consistency. Consistency is that enduring quality of standing together with God throughout the duration of life. Being consistently Christian is more important than all our words combined. Our lives are our best sermons. The world does not need a definition of religion as badly as it needs a demonstration. Brian Harbour, in his book *Living Abundantly,* explains that the consistent Christian worker will be conscientious in three areas. He will be serious in intent, have a singleness of purpose, and practice sincere motives.

When our intention toward our work is serious, we discharge our duties carefully, making sure we do not come up short, that we do not do less than what is expected of our position. A singleness of purpose means carrying out the designated job with an undivided mind, unaffected by petty office rivalries or career-enhancing ploys. Practicing sincere motives ensures a product that is of such quality that we would gladly show it to Jesus Himself and not be ashamed.[10]

As a second-mile Christian in the workplace, you should also be consistently prayerful, consistently honest, consistently industrious, and consistently dependable. St. Francis of Assisi was hoeing his garden when someone asked what he would do if he were suddenly to learn that he would die before sunset. "I would finish hoeing my garden," he replied. An uninterrupted, consistent Christian life is truly the best interpretation and proof of the gospel.

Cooperation. The second-mile Christian lives a surrendered life. Christ is first, others come second, and self last. This person seeks, as well as fosters, a sense of cooperation among his brothers and sisters. Harmony is important because valuable energy is absorbed during times of conflict and dissension. Of course, the second-mile person does not seek unity at the expense of compromise. Moral absolutes do not change even for the sake of harmony, but a sweet spirit of give-and-take in compliant areas separates the person motivated by self from the person controlled by God.

Second-mile Christians have developed a proper attitude toward their jobs. They discharge their duties joyfully, not grudgingly. I talked to a lady recently who was complaining about the numerous duties involved in her job. Her closing statement was the clincher. "My job," she said, "has started to interfere with my life." Knowing that her job consumed an eight-hour chunk of her twenty-four-hour day, I thought to myself, *Lady, your job is your life.* Unless we are contented with our jobs, our attitudes will suffer and we will have very little to contribute that will have lasting value.

Someone has distinguished three kinds of contributors and compared them to the flint, the sponge, and the honeycomb. To get anything out of the flint, you must hammer it, but then you get only chips and sparks. To get water out of a sponge, you must squeeze it; the more pressure you use, the more water you get. But the honeycomb just overflows with its own sweetness. In the workplace, be a honeycomb.

Courtesy. "And so, as those who have been chosen of God, holy and beloved, put on a heart of compassion, kindness, humility, gentleness and patience, bearing with one another" the apostle Paul wrote (Col. 3:12–13).

Nothing costs any less nor goes any farther than the oil of Christian courtesy. True in every area of life, this characteristic prevents a lot of friction—especially in the workplace. No one was kinder or more courteous than Jesus. He, being our example, went out of His way to extend aid and comfort to the weak, the helpless, and the distraught.

Courtesy shows respect and consideration for others. The greater the person, the greater the courtesy. Courtesy is love doing the little things, things that sometimes scarcely seem worth doing, and yet mean so much to those who benefit from them. In the workplace it is lending a hand when someone is over-burdened. It is a cheerful word when a coworker is discouraged. It is a smile and a cheery "Good morning!" when the day is dark and gloomy. Courtesy is often the controlling spring that holds back the slamming office door. It is the salve that soothes jagged nerves and brings gentleness and kindness to the workplace.

Courtesy comes naturally for second-mile Christians. It is the duty the servants of Christ owe to the humblest person with whom they work every day. Jesus said, "To the extent that you did it to one of these brothers of Mine, even the least of them, you did it to Me" (Matt. 25:40).

Common courtesy in the workplace is distinctly Christian. In this push-and-shove generation, courtesy will cause you to stand out in the crowd and direct your coworkers toward Jesus. After all, intimidation and manipulation are poor motivators, but kindness and encouragement emulate the life of Christ.

Reasons for Not Prospering

Some culprits in the workplace may try to sabotage our attempts to please Jesus and prosper professionally. These are fatigue, fatalistic thoughts, discouragement, and disproportionate stress.

Fatigue

Spending too much time on the job without a proper amount of recreation and rest will produce both mental and physical fatigue. With fatigue comes her sisters, anxiety and despair. These two slam the door of blessing in the face of God. They convince us that we are overworked, unappreciated, and misused by management. They steal our fervor and enthusiasm, and they make the workplace a site from which we cannot wait to escape. They make us more concerned with watching the clock than completing the job.

Fatalistic Thoughts

Dr. Victor Frankl, an Austrian psychiatrist, noticed that prisoners did not continue to live very long after they perceived all hope to be gone. Yet his research indicated that even the tiniest ray of hope—the rumor of better food, a whisper about an escape—helped some of the camp inmates to continue living even under dire conditions.[11] Fatalistic thinking creates hopelessness and causes us to begin marking time in our position rather than making a positive contribution. It brings that nagging thought that whispers, "You're not smart enough . . . not educated enough . . . not polished enough . . . not young enough to do this job."

The Roman scholar Cato started to study Greek when he was over eighty years old. When some fatalist asked why he began such a monumental task at his age, he replied, "It's the earliest age I have left." Then he continued with his studies.

If fatalistic thinking is crowding out creativity in your workplace, you must recognize it, call it by name, and then do something to counteract it. Start right where God has placed you, doing what you do best, and then leave the results to Him.

Discouragement

Discouragement, along with his cousins depression and misery, usually visit the workplace when we are striving but not thriving. His tools are the scissors of criticism, the hammer of self-doubt, and the sandpaper of worry. Criticism cuts away our self-respect and dignity, while self-doubt hammers us with questions about our God-given abilities, and worry scrapes back and forth across our mind, making us apprehensive about our future.

Do not allow yourself to be numbered in the ranks of the discouraged. See yourself in the light of God's love and acceptance. Look for the good in people instead of pointing out the worst. Discover what can be done instead of complaining about what cannot. Regard problems, large or small, as opportunities for God to manifest Himself strongly on your behalf. Push ahead, even when it would be easier to quit.

Disproportionate Stress

Ross West, in his book *How to Be Happier in the Job You Sometimes Can't Stand*, lists several elements at work that create stress: too much work to do, work we have not been equipped or trained to handle, confusion concerning job descriptions, too many rules and regulations, the impact of personal life on office affairs, the pressure of making decisions, the way your supervisor relates to you, and the general atmosphere in your work place.[12] Most of this list is caused by one driving force in our lives: the fear of failure. Often our fear of failure—and our frantic attempts to avoid it—cause unnecessary stress in our lives.

Stress comes in two varieties. One mobilizes us for action. It pumps us up for the task at hand and supplies the drive to accomplish the task. However, stress can reach the point that is no longer productive, but destructive, placing our bodies in "distress." Then little irritations become major problems, and thoughts of the job produce a sinking feeling in the stomach, a headache, tight muscles, or a stiff neck.

To combat distress we must replace our fear of failure with faith, the biblical balm for the problems associated with distress. Jesus promised us peace: "My peace I give to you; not as the world gives, do I give to you. Let not your heart be troubled, nor let it be fearful" (John 14:27). Faith sees the invisible, believes the incredible, and receives the impossible even in the workplace. Faith and fear can never exist together. Faith will call attention to fear and help us destroy it before it becomes stress. Faith will not allow us on the bridge of worry and "what might be." Rather it will take us down the paths of "what is" and "what can be."

It has been said that faith in God is the perfect antidote for the fear of men and the creed of circumstances. When fear knocks at the door of your life, let faith open it. Faith makes the up-look good, the outlook bright, and the future glorious. Exercise an active faith in the workplace, and it will bring results. As one worker put it, "Relating one's faith to one's work is like playing a Christian hymn in a minor key. . . . It has a different sound, but you can recognize it."[13]

Vocational Setbacks

A vocational setback does not make you a loser. As Elie Wiesel observed, "According to Jewish tradition, creation did not end with man, it began with him. When He created man, God gave him a secret . . . and that secret was not how to begin, but how to 'begin again.' In other words, it is not given to man to begin; that privilege is God's alone. But it is given to man to begin again." [14]

All of us come to the point where we either make the decision to begin again or quit and give up. When we do not get the job we have prayed for, when the promotion lands in a seemingly less-qualified lap, when the position is terminated or the company folds—we want to give up. Giving up, however, is not an option for the Christian. The apostle Paul gives us a mandate: "We are afflicted in every way, but not crushed; perplexed, but not despairing; persecuted, but not forsaken; struck down, but not destroyed" (2 Cor. 4:8–9). So by the power of God in our lives—we must not, we will not, quit!

Jim Ryun, a devoted Christian, was scheduled to run in the 1972 Olympics in Munich, West Germany. During the 1500-meter race he was proceeding nicely around the track when a runner from Pakistan swerved into Ryun, causing him to fall. When Ryun fell he bumped another runner from Ghana, who also lost his balance. By the time they realized what had happened and got to their feet, the other runners had outdistanced them by several meters. Throwing his hands up in disgust, the runner from Ghana stomped off the track. But not Jim Ryun.

Even though he entertained no hopes of winning, he had no thoughts of quitting. Stunned and injured, he picked his bleeding body up off the track and "began again," placing ninth in the race.

Stay with it! Make up your mind what God wants for your life and get started to accomplish it. Do not let fatigue, fatalistic thinking, discouragement, or vocational setbacks deny you the privilege of prospering in your profession.

"Walk in a manner worthy of the Lord, to please Him in all respects, bearing fruit in every good work " (Col. 1:10).

SEVEN

Firming Up Relationships—Through Forgiveness

Life is a cycling phenomenon.
Nothing stands alone—
No individual, species, or community;
No raindrop, snow crystal, cloud, or stream;
No mountain and no sea.
For in a cycle each thing in one way or another
Is connected with everything else.[1]

She came to me distraught and emotionally bankrupt. "What's wrong with me?" she asked. "I can no longer feel. Somehow I seem to have turned off my emotions and that scares me." Then her voice became a whisper. "I know what the Bible says, pastor. I believe in Jesus. But for some reason I just can't sense Him. I don't feel like a Christian anymore. I don't even feel like a human being."

Childhood Relationships and Battle Fatigue

I knew her background contained many failed relationships. She had experienced great difficulty allowing people to become close to her. Compulsive behavior such as anorexia, bulimia, and depression dogged her every step. When she came to me, her marriage was disintegrating. Experiences had caused her to build an emotional fortress around her life. She seemed determined that no one would penetrate the walls erected around her heart. Why, I asked myself, had this young, attractive woman felt it necessary to disengage herself from all emotional contacts? Why did she feel threatened by personal relationships with others?

Although I was dealing with issues beyond my expertise, I sensed that God wanted me to pray with her. I asked if prayer was a part of her Christian walk, and she declared that she had prayed from the time she was a little girl. "I always prayed when the bad monsters came into my room," she confessed.

While that disclosure sounded strange to me, I dismissed it as no more than childlike language from her past. Starting with the Lord's Prayer in Matthew 6, I began with "Our Father," and asked her to repeat the words after me. There was silence.

When I questioned her hesitation, I discovered that her own father had deserted her when she was a small child, leaving her with the feeling that she was somehow to blame for his exit. Because of this experience she had great difficulty with the concept of God as a faithful, loving, caring Father. As best I could, I tried to explain to her that God was a good Daddy, one who would always be there, and not at all like the earthly daddy she had known. When she seemed to accept that, we started over, laboriously reciting one phrase after another.

> Our Father who art in heaven, hallowed be Thy name.
> Thy kingdom come. Thy will be done,
>   on earth as it is in heaven.
> Give us this day our daily bread.
>   And forgive us our debts,
>   as we also have forgiven our debtors. . . .

Again there was silence. She did not complete the phrase, so I repeated the words "as we forgive our debtors." Still, there was silence. When I raised my head I became aware of a rage boiling up inside this woman that I had not previously encountered in all my experience as a minister. Quietly, resolutely, she said, "I cannot. I will not pray that prayer. You have no right to ask me to pray that today. No one has the right to ask me to do that, not even God. He allowed all those bad things to happen to me, and I will never forgive Him, or them, for what they did to me."

Then, like raw sewage spilling into a flower garden, the events of the past began to pour from her. Her trauma was not some fabricated piece of flotsam dredged up by an overzealous therapist. This was the real thing. The memories had not faded. The monsters in her room had been real. They were her uncles, their male friends, her older brothers—and oh, yes, even her father. Time revealed that she had been sexually abused by most of the men in her family, and she was determined never to trust a man again. Nor could she find it within herself to forgive.

Passed around like yesterday's newspaper, her very soul had been torn open and read by those she should have trusted most, without regard for the sanctity of her spirit. The vicious cycle from childhood had continued into adulthood. She was used and then discarded, only to be picked up by someone else, to be used and discarded again and again. "No!" she said, "I will never forgive them for what they did to me. And, preacher, you have no right to ask me to do that."

The High Price of Forgiveness

Forgiveness is not cheap; it comes with a high price tag. God knows that. All one has to do to verify that fact is to travel outside the walls of Jerusalem to a place called Calvary where Jesus Christ, the Son of God, was crucified for the sins of the world. That was the place where God's forgiveness was forged. No, forgiveness is not cheap. It costs sweat, tears, and sometimes blood. We, however, will never fully experience the refreshing forgiveness of God until we allow Him to forgive others through us. The scars of yesterday's wrongs will not heal. The voices of anger and accusation will not stop, nor will the memories of the wrongs done to us by family, friends, or foes fade unless, in the economy of God's mercy, we learn to forgive those "who have trespassed against us."

Do you remember the story of Camelot, the fairy-tale land where knights were bold, chivalry was the code of conduct, and good always triumphed over evil? It was the place of King Arthur's court. There, it never rained . . . except at night. And in Camelot it was always spring—that is, until Sir Lancelot and Lady Guinevere betrayed King Arthur's love and trust. Then the tranquility was shattered and problems crept into paradise. There was a major breakdown of relationships, and when realism set in, Camelot evaporated into the dream world from which it had come, never to be seen or heard from again.

Sometimes human beings, especially early in their lives, fantasize an existence in that unrealistic "Camelotian Zone." Families develop preconceived ideas concerning the natural order of life in the home, and when expectations for one another plummet, battle fatigue sets in. Just as in those early chapters of Genesis, when the number of people began to increase on planet Earth, so did relational turmoil, confrontation, hostility, and even bloodshed.

Climbing Out of the Pit

When relationships dissolve or turn sour, we may find ourselves in an emotional pit or a psychological prison, a slave to spiritual doubt and despair, bitter and angry with God. There seems to be no help or no future for us. We feel alone and abandoned. We lose hope of ever climbing out on our own.

Dan and Cindy understand the pit. Together they were preparing to fulfill their life's goals. They had been appointed to the mission field to serve God when Cindy was brutally raped. To this day she says, "I cannot get over this thing. It is like a darkness that hangs over my head."

Ruby knows the pit. Her mother tried to abort her. When that failed, she abandoned her. Her father gave her to an aunt, who gave her to a grandmother, who raised her but did not love her. Her grandmother's husband and her uncles repeatedly molested her. She was used as a ritualistic prostitute by people who were Satan worshipers. Later in life, when she tried to straighten out the mess created by years of relational abuse, she was abandoned by her husband and her children. She says, "I cannot get over this. I can't climb out of the pit."

When Jeremiah, the prophet, was in his pit of despair (Lam. 3:1–18), he cried, "God is punishing me. I didn't ask for this. I am physically hurting. I have lost my ability to choose. I have no freedom. God has done this to me. God has deserted me. I was serving Him and I got into trouble for being faithful."

It reminds me of the old Quaker whose fields had just been flooded. He looked up to God and said, "God, I am not surprised that you do not have many friends because of the way you treat the ones you do have." Sometimes life is harsh and it measures out liberal doses of pain, even for God's people. Sometimes even the most spiritual plead with God, "I don't understand! What's going on in my life?"

That must have been the temptation for the young patriarch, Joseph, who encountered numerous relational setbacks. However, the phrase that continually speaks to us in the life of Joseph is not "Why me, God?" but "the LORD was with Joseph" (Gen. 39:2). That phrase epitomizes and characterizes the life of Joseph, the life of Jesus, and, hopefully, your life. Even though he did not always understand God's methods or motives, Joseph knew for a certainty that God was with him, and he trusted—had faith in, relied on, depended totally on—God to work out every area of his life, including relationships. In the good times and bad times, whether people were cursing him or praising him, he was always conscious of God's protective presence. He depended on God to give him the strength to control his actions and reactions, and he trusted God to control the actions and reactions of those around him. "God was with him," and he prospered— in the pit, in slavery, in the prison, and even as prime minister.

Alexander Solzhenitsyn had been in the Gulag, a Soviet prison camp. He had been forced to do back-breaking labor until he came to the point of exhaustion. With little food and little rest, he was constantly watched by guards, never allowed to communicate with another human being.

Never permitted a newspaper or magazine from the outside, he came to believe that he was forgotten by everyone, even God. In his despair, he decided to commit suicide, but he could not reconcile that act with the teachings of the Bible. Then he decided to end his misery by trying an escape, knowing that he would surely be shot. He rationalized that his death would then be at the hands of another and not his own doing.

The appointed day came when he would put his fateful plan into action. Sitting under a tree during a brief respite from work, he glanced at the guards to see where they were positioned. Just as he started to jump and run, a prisoner he had never seen before stood in front of him. Looking into his eyes, Solzhenitsyn said he could see more love than he had ever seen before emanating from the eyes of another human being. The prisoner stooped down with a small twig in his hand and began to draw the symbol of the cross in the soil of Soviet Russia. When Solzhenitsyn saw the cross, he knew God had not forsaken him. He knew God was right there beside him in his deepest pit. Little did he realize that at that very moment, Christians all over the world were praying for his release, and within three days he would be sitting in Geneva, Switzerland, a free man.[2]

"Who is among you that fears the LORD, that obeys the voice of His servant, that walks in darkness and has no light? Let Him trust in the name of the Lord and rely on his God" (Isa. 50:10). When you find yourself in difficulties, do not become bitter with God, accusing Him and insisting that He explain everything to you. While you cannot depend on life to always be kind, or others around you to be understanding, you can depend on God to always be faithful.

By faith, believe that God is trustworthy and loving. He is working out His perfect plan in your life. Do not become a demanding child, insisting that God become accountable to you. "Humble yourselves, therefore, under the mighty hand of God, that He may exalt you at the proper time" (1 Pet. 5:6). When God has ordained the darkness, do not try to kindle your own fire. Wait on the Lord. He will turn your midnight into sunrise, your Calvary into Easter. Look beyond yourself and depend on Him. God is in control, whether you believe it or not, and He knows what He is doing. Trust Him!

Avoid Relational Battle Fatigue

The art of building and maintaining relationships is a lot like riding a ship at sea. Storms come that threaten to sink the ship and blow it off course. But in order to know where you are and where the ship is going, you must constantly look at charts and steer your ship by the stars.

That is not always easy. Far too many lives are being guided by shooting stars rather than by the North Star. Yet the wise seaman prefers the North Star because it doesn't change according to times, customs, or the deliberations of men. It is constant and consistent. Even though the traveler often finds it necessary to correct his own course, he can navigate his life by that which does not change, that which is the same yesterday, today, and forever.

Humanity, the highest creation of God, created in His image, has the ability to hear and understand information, as well as to process that information logically and then make intelligent decisions. Human beings have access to that greatest of all guides for emotional stability, the Bible. While people change, the Word of God remains constant. Our nature, needs, and desires change with age, surroundings, and circumstances. Therefore, it is logical to assume that our relationships will fluctuate because they are always changing.

This is certainly true in my own life. My married daughter, who was once a child, is different from my single daughter, who is no longer a teenager, who is different from my teenage son, who is no longer a baby, who is different from my wife, who is no longer my fiancèe, who is different from my mother, who is no longer my caretaker . . . and the analogy goes on and on. How is it possible then, amid all the confusion, to maintain, build, and move these complex relationships in the right direction?

A Lesson from the Desert

When you leave the ancient city of Jericho and travel up to Jerusalem by the old Jericho Road, you will meander up a dry river bed called the Wadi Kelt. Within that wadi is a deep, foreboding valley called the Valley of the Shadow of Death. It is a dry, arid, desolate place. Apart from tourists, the only sound you will hear is the air that is stirred by a hot, intolerable desert wind or perhaps the occasional bleating of a flock of passing sheep. It is a lonely, solitary place. Nothing thrives there except an old monastery . . . and silence.

This is the place that the psalmist David wrote about when he said, "Even though I walk through the valley of the shadow of death I will fear no evil" (Ps. 23:4). When writing this particular psalm, David may have thought about his past relational failures as a father and husband. There was the failed marriage with Michal, the daughter of his predecessor, King Saul, and the extramarital affair with Bathsheba, followed by her husband's murder.

There were the times when David did nothing about the petty rivalries among the children in his household: the raping of Tamar by her brother Amnon and the killing of Amnon by Absalom. Then there was the rebellion of Absalom as he mounted a successful civil war, wresting the throne from his father and threatening to kill his dad if he got half the chance. David was a successful king and warrior; but as a husband and father, he failed miserably in certain areas. When there is a breakdown in the area of relationships, what can we do? Perhaps, like David, we can find the answer in this ancient valley.

High on the side of the north slope of the barren valley stands a solitary palm tree. A water course from Jerusalem has been directed that way through the desert, and on the jagged precipice of that valley, just before the water plunges down its steep sides, that lone tree has taken root, obviously drawing its nourishment from the moist soil there on the crest of the valley.

As one who has been to Israel on many occasions, I can take a tour bus to the mountain overlooking this valley and see the emptiness and desolation of the terrain below. Then pointing out the tree, I can open my Bible and read from Psalm 1:3, "And he will be like a tree firmly planted by streams of water, which yields its fruit in its season, and its leaf does not wither; and in whatever he does, he prospers."

There on the side of the Valley of the Shadow of Death, where the forces of destruction are so near, stands a promise of hope, a promise of tomorrow. The psalmist reminds us that we must find a stream of water that is steady and dependable.

From that stream comes the "water" necessary for sustaining life. To be the tree that is always thriving as well as surviving, always giving fruit and refreshment to others, always providing shade, our roots must plunge deep into the arid soil of life and find the reliable stream that continues to flow. Just as the life of the tree depends upon the flow of the water cascading into that valley, so we must depend on God for spiritual nourishment in times of relational drought.

When faced with relational breakdowns we must find a spiritual well that will not run dry. We must come to Jesus, the self-confessed "living water" (see John 4) and discover the source of life-giving power and strength that will not stop in times of drought or relational crisis. That eternal spring flows from the Word of God. We must allocate a daily portion of our time to be alone with God in order to drink deeply from the well of God's refreshing love. When we tap into this stream, then our hearts will be nourished and our strength will be made continually new. Only the tree planted by that sure and certain brook will survive the long, hot, dry days of "relational" summer.

If You Are Stuck in the Valley

When I went to a professional basketball game, I was amazed at how quickly the action took place on the court. Caught up in the excitement, I was also becoming quite a sideline coach. I *knew* what the players should do to win the game! But in reality, I had never been where they were, nor had I ever done what they were doing on that court. Likewise, when I am in relational crisis I do not want tips from the stands that "just might" pull me through the game. I want advice from someone who has been there sweating and straining on the floor.

Joseph was such a person. He is one particularly delightful biblical character who embodies the *savoir faire* necessary for successful interpersonal relationships. Somehow Joseph knew how to interact with his parents, siblings, and community. He understood what it took to get along with others.

He took responsibility for his own life. When there were setbacks, he persevered. When there was injustice, he forgave. He knew that God had a plan for his life. Therefore, if Joseph was able to rise above his relational circumstances and live a judicious life, then it is reasonable to assume that it is also possible for us to live that same type life.

Joseph overcame a great deal in his pathway to greatness. His life contained all the elements of a literature classic. There was triumph and tragedy, success, power struggles, intrigue, and in typical fashion, the hero won in the end.

When the story began, it was obvious that Joseph was the favorite of his father's twelve sons. They all had the same father, but there were four different mothers in the family. Joseph's mother, Rachel, was considered the favorite wife of Joseph's father, Jacob. But Leah, Rachel's sister, also had children by Jacob, as did both their handmaids. Talk about confusion! Joseph's half brothers were also his cousins.

This blended family had problems with aggression, jealousy, rivalry, and accountability from the beginning. But as we read the account, we find Joseph taking the eraser of forgetfulness and obliterating the baggage of his life by saying, "The attitudes and actions of others do not determine the outcome of my life. I am responsible for me. I have no excuses. I will be thankful, and by the grace of God, I will overcome the forces of my upbringing and my past. I know that my God is able to accomplish His purpose in me. He will prevail." And God did prevail in Joseph's life.

Neither the physiological or the psychological makeup of his family caused Joseph confusion in the area of his own identity. He knew who he was. Joseph had a strong self-identity because he had deep religious roots, and above all, he knew he was special to both his earthly father and his heavenly Father. Psychologists today tell us that if a child or, for that matter, any person is to be emotionally healthy and stable, he or she must know beyond a shadow of a doubt that a significant someone in their lives is absolutely crazy about them. Joseph observed that kind of love in his earthly father, who made him a multi-colored tunic (see Gen. 37:3–4), but he also experienced that *agape* love flowing from his heavenly Father, who gave him dreams of grandeur (see Gen. 37:5, 9).

Never underestimate the power of love, attention, and unconditional acceptance that flow through the lives of family members. The desire to be loved and accepted will drive a person beyond the boundaries of reality and cause him or her to push all limits just to have a relationship with a sense of belonging and acceptance.

Even lawless gangs become "family" to their members. Within this environment they feel significant. They feel loved and appreciated. The rules are kept simple, and in return they receive loyalty, companionship, recognition, and admiration. Interestingly enough, those are the same common components that everyone needs to find in relationships. Those are the elements that ward off relational battle fatigue.

How did Joseph overcome without a support system, with no one to encourage him, no one to lead him, and no political connections? The Bible tells us that early in Joseph's life God revealed that he would one day be in a position of authority. Joseph chose to believe God, and that belief kept him afloat in the angry sea of life's uncertainties. God gave him a plan and a promise, and then God gave him the opportunity to work out that plan in the relational pits of his own life.

You, too, can have power to overcome when you find yourself in that pit if you remember these simple principles.

- Have faith in God, knowing He is always there.
- Believe the Word, that God loves and cares for you.
- Discover God's plan for your life by reading His Word.
- Continue serving Him, no matter what.

> Turn everything over to God in prayer.

Living with Relational Adversity

Adversity, the battleground of life, can make us stronger, but it also has the potential to destroy us. It can make us better or bitter. In Joseph's life there was much relational adversity. He was hated by his brothers, who sensed their father's favoritism toward him, but he refused to hate back. They sold him into slavery, but Joseph would not be the slave of hatred and bitterness. In Egypt he was lied to, lied about, and betrayed. He was falsely accused of trying to rape his master's wife and, even though he was innocent of all charges, he was thrown into prison. During this time of relational disillusion —when he must have thought everyone, including family, friends, and community, had turned against him—he may have come dangerously close to suffering from battle fatigue. That helpless hopelessness pulls you into a dark hole and imprisons you there. But Scripture tells us that through all of this Joseph never doubted God's love for him and he never forgot his love for his family. He made a conscious decision that he would not throw in the towel, but rather he would believe God to fulfill the dreams of his life.

Are you wrestling with hatred and bitterness right now? Perhaps it is against a family member: an abusive mom or dad, an unkind sister or brother, or an ungrateful, unlovable child. Like Joseph, does it seem as if you are in the middle of nowhere, and people have forgotten you? I remember, as a young pastor in the coalfields of eastern Kentucky, I too felt that I had been abandoned by God. I so desperately wanted to broaden my ministry and pastor in an area where I could reach more people for Christ. Yet it seemed the opportunity always passed me by. I saw others promoted. Pulpit committees came, but they never stayed.

Then one spring, during a revival meeting being held in my little church, the visiting evangelist began to encourage me. "Joe," he said, "I know you think that you are back up here in these mountains and everyone has forgotten you, and you think no one knows where you are. Well, I want to tell you something. God knows where you are, and He has not forgotten you."

Something happened to me when he said those words. My life was instantly energized. My ministry took on fresh meaning as I continued working there in the mountains, knowing my Father's watchful eye was ever upon me. And that was Joseph's secret. He knew four things. First, he knew God was aware of his situation. Second, he realized God knew his exact location. Third, he knew where God was, and fourth, he knew how to get in touch with Him.

Are you fatigued by the perception that you are going it alone, or even that you are rowing your life upstream against the whole world? Then you need to be refreshed by this thought: God knows where you are and He is aware of the circumstances surrounding your life. He has not forgotten you. Because of that you can put your roots deep within the soil of His Word and drink long and deep from the river of water that never runs dry.

Life is not always pleasant. We are in constant danger of developing relational fatigue as we deal with our children, our coworkers, our community, our friends, and our extended family. Every relationship will have down times, but we can depend on God, whose very name, "I Am," means He is sufficient to handle each test and trial we might encounter.

Every relationship comes to a crossroads where we can either become bitter and quit or move on. We can ask for a divorce. We can quit and walk away from our spouse, our job, our family, our friends. But if we believe in God, if we believe He has a wonderful plan for our lives, if He is active and working there right now, we will have the strength to stay the course and finish the journey. Rather than blaming God for our relational problems, we must start believing Him for His solutions. We must start claiming the power and promises of God for our lives. We must refuse to live under the condemnation of failure, fatigue, and ruptured relationships. We must get into the Word of God and discover who He is.

Find out for yourself what His plan is for your life and discover how He is going to implement that plan through you to benefit others. Start living according to the revelation of God rather than desiring retaliation, retribution, and revenge. Live your life according to His principles, rather than basing every decision on the pain of the moment. Get an eternal view of life and realize that God's relationship with you will last forever and He is close by, enabling you to live in harmony with the ones you hold dear.

Avoid Quick Fixes for Relationships

It took God only six days to create the world, but you are more important to Him than worlds. So He will take as much time as necessary to work out the relationships in your life. You are the most delicate of all His creations, precious in His sight, and He will mold and shape you so that you and your brother, sister, wife, children, or friends can lovingly coexist.

The great pianist Paderewski was about to perform a concert in a certain music hall. A woman who liked his music came, forcing her small son to accompany her. The boy was obviously uninterested in the music and unimpressed by the great pianist. Before the distracted mother knew it, her child had broken away and rushed to the stage. There, to the horror of the audience, he awkwardly seated himself at the piano and started playing the simple tune "Chop Sticks."

Hearing the commotion from his dressing room, Paderewski looked out and recognized the crisis brewing in the child's life. Paderewski calmly walked onto the stage, stood behind the little boy, and began a lovely, haunting accompaniment to the simple tune, while he whispered in the child's ear, "Don't stop. Keep on playing. Keep on playing." The melody ended with a standing ovation and a call for an encore.

That same "principle of continuation" illustrates the life of Joseph. He knew that, no matter how circumstances looked, God would never leave him or forsake him. He had learned that the lovingkindness of God was a loyal love that could not be won or lost.

He had heard the footsteps of God walking beside him as the slave caravan lethargically made its way across the sand toward Egypt. Joseph heard the tender whisper of God as he stood naked and humiliated on the auction block. When he became the common property of a rich Egyptian, it was God who was his constant companion. Echoing through the stench and clamor of Pharaoh's prison, he heard the voice of God resounding, "I am the Conductor of the concert of your life. Keep playing; keep loving; keep believing. I am behind you, in front of you, and within you, and I will fill in the missing orchestration of your life. Just be patient and give Me time to do it."

And Joseph believed God. Whether he was thrown in a pit, sold into slavery by his brothers, or placed in a dungeon for a crime he did not commit—Joseph always found God in those dark relational places of his life, and that enabled him to pick up the damaged dreams and move on. Joseph refused to give up on God and Joseph refused to give up on people. He decided to serve them rather than hate them.

Replace Hatred with Service

In Genesis 45 we find a most moving portion of Scripture. There we witness the sovereignty of God as He brought Joseph and his brothers back together after years of alienation and separation. Joseph stood in front of them, having been elevated by God to the lofty position of prime minister of Egypt, in charge of food storage and distribution. A dreadful famine in the land of Palestine had reunited him with the same brothers who kidnapped and sold him into slavery so many years ago. As prime minister, it was Joseph who was now in the position of power. As Joseph had once begged for life and freedom from the pit, now his brothers assumed the posture of beggars as they sought food for their starving families from a man they recognized only as an ominous, powerful stranger. Here was his chance. Joseph could now exact his revenge upon them. It was certainly within his power. But he chose to love and forgive them, moving beyond the offenses of the past.

And that is what you have to do in order to break free of relational battle fatigue. You have to make a conscious decision to move beyond the circumstances that cause you to hate the one who now imprisons you in that hatred; move beyond that broken relationship with your lover; move beyond that argument with your neighbor; move beyond that conflict with your boss; move beyond that disagreement with your child. Forgive them and then forgive yourself.

Facets of Forgiveness

After all the hardships and heartaches caused by the direct actions of his brothers, how was Joseph able to forgive?

- He forgave privately. Forgiveness is between the party offended and the offender (Gen. 45:1). When he revealed his identity to his brothers, he first cleared the room of outsiders. The process of forgiveness is a private matter.
- He forgave with his heart as well as his mind (Gen. 45:2). He wept before them, revealing the mercy, compassion, and tenderness still in his heart toward his family.

  During the process of seeking or receiving forgiveness,

be genuine and open. Express sorrow and love. Those emotions allow others to deal authentically with you.

> He forgave by confronting the past. You cannot run away from the past (Gen. 45:3). The very presence of Joseph revealed his brothers' past sins and forced them to deal with the consequences of their actions.

The rift that has taken place between you and another individual should not be disregarded and ignored, but sensibly and calmly recognized and brought to the surface. You need to begin to reestablish a sense of honesty and sincerity as you deal with the barriers between you.

Like Joseph's brothers, we must learn to deal with the consequences of our actions, especially as they impact others around us. They, being older, had the responsibility of leadership and accurately representing their father. Yet because of their selfish and resentful actions, they betrayed their own brother and broke their aging father's heart, causing him to live much of his life in sorrow and despair.

In an incident in Southern California an aerospace executive left his family and walked away from the corporate world because he said he "felt trapped." "Never become too good at something you hate," he told his fellow workers shortly before leaving his job, "or they will make you do it the rest of your lives." He had created his own private hell because he valued things above people and his soul had been invaded by a vast emptiness and an immeasurable restlessness.

Then he did what many have thought about doing. He simply walked away and for the next seven years he wandered the beaches of California as a vagabond. He had made his escape from responsibility, family, and job. Back home, however, there was a devastated family that had once depended on him.

Exhibiting their shallowness, his coworkers called him a hero and threw a party each year to celebrate his escape from reality. But he is no hero. A hero does not walk away from relational responsibility. Real heroes confront life with all its terrors and ambiguities and work to change the things that they find impossible to tolerate.

Joseph did not quit on life. He chose to forgive privately and passionately, confronting the demons of his past. And that is the way you must forgive.

> He forgave his brothers before being asked (Gen. 45:3). Joseph's brothers were speechless with fear when they recognized him, but their reaction did not impede his resolve to forgive. Even though they had not requested his forgiveness, Joseph knew that in order to get on with God's purpose for his life the barrier between himself and his brothers had to be broken down.

  The responsibility for forgiveness rests with the Christian. Whether you are the offender or the offended, you are required to initiate the healing process.

> He was tender toward those needing forgiveness (Gen. 45:5). Joseph honestly acknowledged their mistake, but also explained his understanding of God's greater purpose for all their lives, thereby eliminating their need to continue carrying the tremendous burden of incapacitating guilt.

  Heaping guilt at the feet of the offender only slows the process of forgiveness. Indeed God can make lemonade out of lemons if given half a chance; He can bring joy out of sadness. The person who acts with tenderness becomes a healing salve and saves a relationship.

> He forgave without being bitter (Gen. 45:5,7). Joseph realized that everything in his life had taken place in order for God to preserve his people. He was therefore able to submit himself to God and accept His greater plan. Joseph knew nothing touched him that wasn't first sifted through God's love and mercy. His relationship to God was vitally

more important than petty revenge and bitterness.

Remember, nothing touches you that has not already touched God. Look at life through His all-encompassing eyes. He sees the bigger picture. Trust Him and do not become bitter. Let Him help you forgive.

A study questionnaire was sent to several hundred counselors and pastors. The question was asked, "What problems are you seeing most often among your counselees?" The response most repeated was bitterness. People who are bitter feel intense animosity and are often emotionally exhausted. They are suffering from battle fatigue. Bitterness—that resentful, often hostile emotion—takes and takes and takes from its victim, sapping them of revitalizing energy. Bitter people often set their one goal in life as getting even and are paralyzed in that dimension, forfeiting any kind of future creative activity in their lives.

One man planned for years to kill his adversary out of revenge for a past injustice. Finally, he succeeded in his task. In prison he was asked how he felt now that his retaliation was complete. His pathetic reply was, "It wasn't enough. He only died once, but I still have to die every day. I wish I could bring him back alive and kill him over and over again every day to make him pay for what he did to me."

If you are bitter toward a family member, friend, or coworker, you fantasize about getting even. You make statements, spread gossip, and find ways to exact revenge. As Theodore Roosevelt once said, "Always give your best, never get discouraged, never be petty, and always remember, others may hate you, but those that hate you don't win unless you hate them and then you destroy yourself."

> He forgave so God's greater plan could be accomplished (Gen. 45:7–8). If Joseph harbored bitterness, his attitude would have kept him in prison. If he remained in prison, his nation might have slowly starved in the wilderness of

Palestine. Joseph would have missed the blessing of being the instrument God used for their physical salvation.

To overcome bitterness try to look beyond your present circumstances and trust God to bring a greater good from your situation.

> He forgave and brought blessings to his brothers (Gen. 45:9–15). When Joseph's brothers moved past their own fear and accepted his authentic forgiveness, their emotional and physical needs were met. They received food for themselves and their families. They experienced a newfound sense of security and safety under Joseph's protection.

The act of forgiving and accepting forgiveness releases us from relational battle fatigue and frees us to become all God intended under His umbrella of protection and provision.

> He forgave and was reunited with those he loved (Gen. 45:10–11). Joseph's unconditional forgiveness brought his family and his nation back together in a place where God could meet all their needs. He was reunited with his aging father, who had thought him dead. The family lived out their days together, and the nation was preserved. It all happened because Joseph allowed God to work in and through his life. He did not become bitter nor was he unforgiving.

When you allow God to forgive through you, lives are redirected and broken relationships are reunited.

In the early part of this century, Gitz Rice, a famous Canadian composer and songwriter, joined the Canadian regiment and was sent to Europe during World War I. There he was stationed with his piano in the grim no-man's land between the German and French forces.

On Christmas Eve, 1917, a piano was brought to the front lines and in the stillness of the night, Christmas carols could be heard up and down the trenches by Canadians as well as Germans. Around midnight, Rice played "Silent Night." Canadian troops sang out from the trenches. When Rice paused for a moment, all were surprised to hear the Germans also singing "Stille Nacht, Heilige Nacht." Other carols were sung, first by one side and then the other. The weary soldiers sang until first light. Then sadly, hostilities resumed.

Wouldn't it be wonderful if everyone could come out of the trenches of relational "wars," put all differences aside, and sing together the praises of the One who makes that "heavenly peace" possible? The call is to first do our part to firm up relationships and put this world back together by forgiving.

E I G H T

Surviving when Your Brook Dries Up

The dark threads are as needful in the
Weaver's skillful hand,
As the threads of gold and silver in the
Pattern He has planned.[1]

I received the following letter from Steven's mother. It serves as a good example of how fragile happiness in this life can be.

Dear Pastor,

1968 was not a very good year for healthy young American men. I will always remember the day Steven left for Vietnam. He looked so dashing in his uniform, a six-foot-one-inch paratrooper, weighing 195 pounds. He seemed so invincible. I was proud to be his mother, and his dad was just as proud as I was. I couldn't help but think about the day he was born. We were so incredibly happy. He was our third child, our only son, and we loved him so.

I can't say those days when he was in Vietnam were easy for any of us, but they did pass quickly and Steven was good about writing. I could read danger between the lines of his letters, but I never let my fears show through when I wrote him back.

Then it came—that horrible yet wonderful news. He's seriously wounded, but still alive. And Steven was on his way back to the States. Neither his dad nor I spoke on the way to the airport to pick him up. There was an identifiable, unspoken tension in the car. We had been separated from him for so long. What could we expect? I thought I had prepared myself for the meeting, but as it turned out, I hadn't.

His face told the whole story. That look of brave confidence and carefree frivolity had vanished, replaced by a gaunt, haunted expression that had supplanted all sense of confidence and self-assurance. His clothes hung on his bony frame at odd angles. He had lost so much weight. He tried to put up a good front, tried to be positive, but as I reached for him there in the airport, the man I had sent away trembled and collapsed, and all that was left was my frightened little boy.

It was during this time that Steven and his dad became very close. Jack spent every waking hour with him. In his weakened condition he needed constant attention and supervision. I'll never forget the day Steven felt strong enough to attempt his first shower after arriving home. We helped him into the master bathroom where Dad stood waiting with a towel. He left Steven for just a moment to collect fresh pajamas. When he returned, Steven was standing naked in front of a full length mirror, noticeably horrified by his scarred, emaciated body.

The ugly red scars made initially by bullets, then accentuated by surgeon's scalpels, glared back at him. There were hollow places where muscle and tissue had once given shape to an almost perfect body. Some of his bones were noticeably disfigured. A haunted, whimpering cry was coming from his throat, "Oh my God, Daddy! Look! Just

> look what they've done to me. Look, Daddy! Look what they've done to me!"
>
> Pastor, I had done pretty well up to that point. I had operated on energy I didn't know I possessed. But when I heard my boy crying—and I couldn't do anything to make him stop hurting—I ran out of resources. My brook finally dried up.

Has your brook ever dried up?

If this terminology is confusing, let me refer you to a portion of Scripture in 1 Kings 17 where Elijah, the faithful prophet of God, obediently rested by the brook Cherith. The brook provided for him during a predicted two-and-one-half-year drought. The Bible says Elijah "did according to the word of the Lord, for he went and lived by the brook Cherith, which is east of the Jordan. And the ravens brought him bread and meat in the morning and bread and meat in the evening, and he would drink from the brook" (1 Kings 17: 5–6).

What a beautiful example of one man's obedience to God. I can almost see Elijah squatting there beside that trickling brook, scooping up handfuls of sparkling water, quenching his thirst, washing his dusty face, praising the God of heaven for his safe haven. Daily he sat by the stream, slept by the stream, prayed by the stream—never venturing far from its life-giving source. Then one day, he noticed a slight reduction in its output. Perplexed and confused, he watched as his beloved stream dwindled to a trickle, then to a dribble, and finally "after a while, the brook dried up, because there was no rain in the land" (1 Kings 17:7).

But wait! Was it not God who withheld the rain in the first place? Was it not God who sent Elijah, His prophet, to herald the drought message in the courts of Ahab, the king? And was it not God who commanded Elijah to "Go away . . . and hide yourself by the brook Cherith" (1 Kings 17:3)? Does it not seem logical that such an all-powerful God would have little trouble keeping Elijah's tiny stream flowing? God promised; Elijah obeyed; but the brook eventually went dry anyway. Why?

What about Jonah, the reluctant missionary? After sloshing around in the belly of a "great fish," he decided to obey God's call to preach to the pagan Ninevites. After a successful evangelistic crusade through the city—where every man, woman, boy, and girl in Nineveh repented and turned from their wickedness—the pouting preacher retreated to a nearby hillside. As he sullenly suffered in the heat, God mercifully provided him protection from the sun by allowing a plant to grow up over his head. Basking in God's provision, Jonah reclined. Content in his newly found oasis, he slept.

But overnight a worm attacked his beloved plant "and it withered" (Jonah 4:7). Then a scorching east wind started to blow, and as the sun rose over Nineveh the next morning, it beat down with fresh vigor on Jonah's sunburned head. Puzzled, he screamed, "Why has this happened to me? Don't play games with me, God. I did what you wanted me to do. I didn't like it, but I did it, and now I'm the one who is suffering. Just kill me, and be done with it!"

Then there was Abraham, who waited one hundred years to hold his baby son, Isaac—only to hear these words from God: "Take now your son, your only son, whom you love, Isaac, and go to the land of Moriah; and offer him there as a burnt offering on one of the mountains of which I will tell you" (Gen. 22:2). In obedience Abraham responded and set off to destroy the very one who had brought life to his dreams.

Yet every time the leather on the soles of his sandals hit the loose stones scattered about Mount Moriah, his flesh must have silently cried out, "Why, God? I followed You faithfully all these years. Why, God? I believed You, even when all hope was gone. Why, God? Have I done something to displease You? Have You deserted me? Don't You love me any more?"

No amount of reasoning could make sense out of this request. After all, did God not promise and then provide Abraham's son? Had he and Sarah not faithfully held on to their faith while waiting those long years for God to give them an offspring? When he was born, had they not cherished him, nurtured him, taught him to love and trust God? Would God give such a gift and then suddenly reclaim it? It did not make sense to Abraham—and sometimes the twists and turns of our lives don't make any sense to us either.

Now, let me ask you that question again. Has your brook dried up? Do you sometimes become fatigued by the tremendous amount of energy required just to pick up the pieces and move on? Are there reminders of broken dreams, broken hearts, and broken lives cluttering the intersections of your life? Do they make it impossible for you to smile and really mean it? Have you questioned God's love, God's compassion, or God's availability in your life? Have circumstances unleashed an avalanche of doubt in your heart and caused your faith to shake and crumble under the enormous pressure?

Is it possible that whatever you depended on most, whatever brought you the most joy, whatever gave your life meaning somehow disappeared, and you have been left feeling empty, hopeless, and helpless? Perhaps it disappeared through no fault of your own while you were obediently serving God, faithfully doing His will. Things seemed fine and secure; then one day the bottom fell out of your world, and the stream dried up. And for the first time you saw yourself a vulnerable, defenseless person, spinning frantically out of control, totally unequipped to cope with the realities and challenges of life.

Viewing Life from Heaven's Perspective

I believe it is important for Christians to admit that sometimes bad things do happen to saved people. The Bible is replete with details from the lives of mistreated, persecuted and martyred saints, people who were faithfully serving God, yet experienced dire tribulation and upheaval in their personal lives. To my knowledge, there is not one greatly used saint who has not had his or her spiritual life fortified by some "faith-shaking experience."

Examine the evidence. David spent time in the valley of the shadow of death and went down in history as Israel's greatest king. Moses spent forty years on the back side of the desert. Then with the staff of God in his hand, he delivered a nation from bondage. Daniel spent time in a den filled with hungry lions. Then he rose from that pit to reveal God's prophetic world plan to future generations. Samuel spent his life apart from his mother and family, faithfully serving in God's house. God allowed him to anoint kings.

Esther spent time in prayer and fasting before she petitioned the king. She was then able to save a nation from sure annihilation. Job spent time in sackcloth and ashes, his body covered with painful boils. Then he experienced the bounteous blessings of God on his life. John, the beloved apostle, spent time in exile on the island of Patmos. Then he penned the Book of the Revelation of Jesus Christ. The apostle Paul spent time in prison writing letters that turned out to be the bulk of the New Testament. Some read like this:

> To this present hour we are both hungry and thirsty, and are poorly clothed, and are roughly treated, and are homeless; and we toil, working with our own hands; when we are reviled, we bless; when we are persecuted, we endure; when we are slandered, we try to conciliate; we have become as the scum of the world, the dregs of all things, even until now.
>
> I do not write these things to shame you, but to admonish you as my beloved children. . . . I exhort you therefore, be imitators of me.
>
> — 1 Corinthians 4:11–14, 16

Viewing life from heaven's perspective seems simple enough—after the fact. For instance, with a thorough investigation of 1 Kings, chapter 17, it is obvious to us that Elijah's brook dried up because it was time for him to move on.

God knew that while he had the brook to depend on, he would never leave Cherith and never accomplish God's purpose for his life. So the stream gradually dwindled and Elijah placed his trust back where it belonged—in God. Then he was able to move on.

What about Jonah? God taught that stubborn fellow a lesson about His mercy and grace toward all people. God knew Jonah was more concerned with his own comfort than the possible annihilation of the entire city of Nineveh. So God put a little "heat" on him to redirect his attention away from himself, toward others.

In Abraham's case, his devotion was tested when God asked him to sacrifice his son, Isaac. Abraham's unquestioned obedience proved his love and faithfulness toward God and provided coming generations an unmistakable picture of the tremendous sacrifice He would make in the future.

But what about Steven, the soldier mentioned earlier in this chapter who sacrificed his future for a cause that many in this country may still deem questionable? What about his mom and dad, who suffer with him on a daily basis? Where was God when the bullets penetrated his young body? One minute's delay could have defrayed the inevitable catastrophe; one sneeze, one snapping twig could have alerted Steven to the impending danger. Where was God? What purpose could He possibly have had in allowing life to run its dreadful course that day in the jungle of Vietnam?

Have you noticed, viewing life from heaven's perspective is not so simple when the story is still in process. We cannot skip to the end of the book and find out why things happened to us or those we love. That is the dilemma each succeeding generation of Christians faces. We observe, and sometimes even understand the purpose of trials and tribulations in the lives of others who have lived before us. But drawing similar conclusions when life is turning the heat up on *us*—well, that's a different matter entirely.

The Dangers of "Feel Good" Theology

Confusion develops when Christians imbibe a "feel good" pseudotheology that imprisons God in a "magic lamp mentality" and forces Him, "in Jesus' name," to grant all our wishes. Creator God is reduced to a cosmic genie waiting on the fringes of eternity, anxious to materialize and make us happy and comfortable.

This pseudotheology has been fostered in large part by greedy, well-dressed charlatans posing as ministers of the gospel. They prance across well-manicured stages in studios that masquerade as churches. They work themselves into a fervor waving an oversized Bible that they rarely take time to open. Dabbing dripping foreheads, they misquote and misrepresent the Word of God to a generation of McDonald's-style Christians who, in turn, expect—even demand—instant spiritual gratification.

These so-called representatives of the gospel of Jesus Christ use His name tritely, take His precepts lightly, and exploit His promises superficially. Their actions undermine the very nature of God. His purpose is to make us holy, not happy.

The apostle Paul said, "For to you it has been granted for Christ's sake, not only to believe in Him, but also to suffer for His sake" (Phil. 1:29). Suffering is a concept that is foreign to this modern brand of feel-good religion. Yet it has permeated authentic Christianity from the first century until the present.

We are confused and fatigued because we expend valuable time and energy imbibing an empty gospel that is alien to the teachings of Christ. He never promised material wealth. He never promised healing from every disease. While He did heal many with a simple touch of His hand or a word spoken from His lips, He had it within His power to abolish all sickness from the face of the entire earth, yet He did not. He did not promise an easy life for His followers. As a matter of fact, His instructions were, "Pick up your cross and follow me."

Any message or messenger that distorts the gospel of Jesus Christ is an instrument of death to those who listen and ingest that pseudogospel. Jesus calls such messengers whitewashed sepulchers, pretty containers filled with death (Matt. 23:27).

Their tactics remind me of the Buchenwald death camp during World War II. The camp was flanked by a clean, white wall with green, manicured lawns where smiling, healthy, innocent-looking girls often played lawn games. Hanging on the wall was a huge sign that read, "Work Means Freedom." But behind those whitewashed walls were gas ovens and torture chambers where men did to other human beings that which is still incomprehensible.

Those Christians who have been manipulated by religious con men with this name-it-and-claim-it theology, this enough-faith-cures-all mentality, will have a difficult time making sense of the message of Jesus.

Perhaps it is time that modern-day Christians rediscover the real Jesus. Accepting Him as He is presented by the Word of God is much less fatiguing than trying to remake Him to fit a particular brand of theology. Unless we discover who He is, what He stands for, and what His purpose is, we will never be able to deal with the unresolved whys of our lives.

A Crisis of Faith

When crisis comes and unresolved whys begin to twist our thinking, theological collapse may be imminent.

Unresolved "Whys"

Unresolved whys are all the questions you have asked God that have not been answered to your satisfaction. For instance, immature Christians often have used verses such as John 14:14 ("If you ask Me anything in My name, I will do it") to entice God to meet their needs by indiscriminately throwing around an incantation involving Jesus' name. They will have many unresolved whys in their lives when material desires are not instantly fulfilled.

Legitimate whys also trouble mature Christians: "Why, God, can't I have children when millions are being carelessly aborted every year in America? Why do I have to grow up in a family where my father is an alcoholic and sexually abuses me when my best friend, who isn't even a Christian, has a loving father? Why am I the only boy in my fifth-grade class whose mom died with cancer this year? Why was my seventeen-year-old daughter raped? Why can't I form a lasting relationship with someone who will take away this terrible loneliness I feel? Why was I born with a birth defect? Why was my only son, a high school senior, killed in a freak car accident? Why did my husband leave me and the kids? Why am I dying? Why, God? Why?

Theological Collapse

Throughout my twenty-plus years of ministry I have not been able to answer these questions and a million more questions just like them. All Christians have them, the unresolved whys. How we choose to deal with them determines whether or not our theology—what we believe about God—is strong. The same is true of theological collapse. For our own purposes we will define "theological collapse" as that period in our lives when our view of who God is does not equate with how He is responding to our circumstances. Theological collapse, therefore, is a rift in fellowship—not relationship—

between God and man that is precipitated by man. It occurs when God does not meet our particular expectations of Him.

Stages that Test Faith

When a crisis touches the Christian's life and is not resolved quickly, a process begins that, if handled incorrectly, may culminate in temporary, or even prolonged, "theological collapse." I believe a crisis takes a Christian through four distinct stages that both test and reshape faith.

Confusion About Your Circumstances

When calamity strikes or bad news is received, the Christian must deal first with shock. At this point one of two reactions takes place. The first and most typical reaction is the one we observe in Job 2:9, when Job's wife, frustrated by the loss of her family and fortune, advises her husband—who, by the way, is afflicted with boils from the soles of his feet to the crown of his head—to "Curse God and die!" She knew that Job had been a just man according to the world's standards, and she could not understand why God had allowed catastrophe after catastrophe to fall on their household. It is as if she expected their relationship with God to serve as a sort of "natural disaster insurance policy," eliminating trials and hardships from life.

In the early stages of dealing with crisis, this is the most common reaction: "Why has God allowed this terrible thing to happen to our family? We have served Him faithfully for years. Is this the thanks we get? We don't deserve this!"

I once heard a fable concerning a large pumpkin and a tiny acorn. It seems a man walked through a forest meditating on the goodness of God, when he looked up and was astounded by the size of a great oak tree. As he pondered its size, he noticed a tiny acorn on one of the branches. At the same time, looking down at his feet, he saw an insignificant vine. Near its end was a huge orange pumpkin. Perplexed by the enigma, he thought, *This is stupid. A tiny acorn on such a huge tree . . . a large pumpkin on such a tiny vine. Why, if I'd been around during creation, I could have straightened out this blunder.*

With that presumptuous statement he laid down to rest under the huge oak. However, his sleep was soon interrupted when that tiny acorn struck him squarely between the eyes, causing him to awaken and cry out in pain from the impact. Then he realized, "What if that had been a pumpkin falling from the tree instead of an acorn? Why, I would most likely be dead." And as he walked away from the base of the tree, pondering the wisdom of the Almighty, he repeated the phrase over and over again to himself, "Whatever God does, God does well."

At times in all our lives, circumstances and events do not turn out as we wish. During those times of crisis we cry out: "This is all wrong! It's not fair! It shouldn't be happening this way!" It's during these times that we must believe with all our heart that God knows what He is doing, and whatever God does, God does well.

This brings us to the second way of reacting to crisis. It's the way Job himself reacted to his catastrophic losses and his own personal illness. In response to his wife's plea to curse God and die, Job said to her, "You speak as one of the foolish women speaks. Shall we indeed accept good from God and not accept adversity?" (Job 2:10). Somehow Job knew that God was still present in his life even when circumstances and common sense indicated otherwise.

Job's unpretentious trust in God reminds me of the little lad who was flying his kite on a cloudy day when the kite disappeared behind an ominous black cloud. Standing alone, appearing to passersby to be holding onto an empty string, the lad was questioned by an elderly man about what he was doing.

"Why, I'm flying a kite," he said boldly.

"I don't see a kite," remarked the puzzled old gentleman.

"Neither do I," replied the child, "but I know it's up there 'cause every now and then I feel a tug on the string."

Job knew God was there because he had already experienced God's tug on his life. Because He had been there in the past, Job trusted God to be there in his present—and his future, even when his future was doubtful. Indeed he had been blessed by God, but he did not presume on God for the perpetual continuation of those blessings. As Christians, we get in trouble when we *accept* God's blessings, then *expect* God's blessings, then *demand* God's blessings, forgetting that they are a privilege, not a right. Job gave God the option to send blessing or adversity, trusting God to do what was beneficial for his life at the time. And he did not dictate the outcome. Nor did he blackmail God by threatening a loss of his affection or allegiance. Listen to these words of confidence from the lips of this faithful, suffering servant of God, "Though He slay me, I will hope in Him" (Job 13:15).

Faith to the Rescue

During stage two faith kicks in, either manipulating faith or submissive faith. Manipulating faith is really not faith in God, but faith in "faith."

Some theological circles measure faith just as we measure sugar, by the spoonful, cupful, or bagful. According to this brand of theology, if we come up short on faith during a crisis, we will almost certainly see our prayers ignored and our petitions before God denied. This cruel ideology relegates God to the status of a divine accountant, adding points when faith is strong, subtracting them when faith is weak. It would have us believe that enough faith manipulates God to grant all our desires and wishes, while too little faith relegates us to face the crisis alone.

I have seen godly parents, crushed under the weight of losing a child, simply told by these manipulators that they just "hadn't had enough faith to pull the child through." This train of thought removes God's will from every situation and places the burden of whether or not prayer is answered on the backs of His powerless children, who, by the way, are further weakened by their debilitating circumstances. God has no part in this performance-based theology. Jesus said, "If you have faith as a [tiny] mustard seed, [living, connected, growing faith], you shall say to this mountain, 'Move from here to there,' and it shall move; and nothing [within the will of God] shall be impossible to you" (Matt. 17:20).

Submissive faith, on the other hand, is more inclined to allow God to be God. Harold Myra, in his book *Living By God's Surprises*, observed, "At the heart of the obedient life is submission to the sovereignty of God . . . even when in the valley of the shadow of death, even when the darkness of the forest around us oppresses, even when we find ourselves in a wilderness experience face to face with the devil himself. Even in the dark we seek to trust the sovereignty and ultimate vindication of the love of God."[3]

This kind of faith—this believing that God is still at work in our lives, even when common sense and dire circumstances tell us otherwise—is submissive faith. It is staking all that we are and everything we have on the One not seen. It is believing God's promises when they are not evident in our lives. It is accepting the awesome truth as stated by Creath Davis, in his book *Lord, If I Ever Needed You It's Now,* "that at some point God's healing mercies for our bodies cease and His grace for dying begins."[4]

Hebrews 11:6 stresses the importance of properly placed faith: "Without faith it is impossible to please Him, for he who comes to God must believe that He is, and that He is a rewarder of those who seek Him." This verse contains two important principles. First, we discover that God Himself is the object of true faith: "he who comes to God must believe that He is." Although basic, this principle is often disregarded.

To be effective, faith must rest in a higher power than ourselves, not a lower one. In order to make a difference in our lives and throughout eternity, faith must rest not in the created, but in the Creator.

Second, we find that God is the rewarder of those who seek Him. The natural tendency is to casually glance at Hebrews 11:6, see the word "rewarder," and imagine God handing out all kinds of material perks, healing our diseases, and immediately solving our problems. That is not the case at all. God is working in us through the trials of our lives to produce spiritual rewards, not temporal, and eternal glory, not physical and material rewards.

Frustration with the Father

Harold Myra also noted,

> There is enigma and paradox in life. There is darkness and then there are flashes of light. How many pious, godly souls have been struck down through the centuries, even as they prayed for deliverance? Yet despite all this . . . despite the impossible questions, the drab and the tawdry times, the failures . . . we are still called upon to pray with, of all things, Great Expectations! An absurdity. A paradox. Yet the gospel truth. God, it seems, chooses to work in enigma and pain, with miracles as rare but as real as meteor flashes across a dark sky.[5]

When Christians fail to yield to His sovereignty, their ultimate reward is frustration if God does not come to the rescue. "If there is a God, He isn't helping me. I must have done something to displease Him." Or, "If there is a God, He must have lost control or He would have changed my circumstances. If there is a God, He must be powerless to do anything about my problem." Or, "If there is a God, He obviously doesn't care what's going on in my life. I'm not important to Him."

How different were Jim and Elisabeth Eliot's reactions to catastrophe when, three times during their first year of missionary work with a small tribe of Indians called the Colorados, they lost everything. Elisabeth's words are recorded in Russell Chandler's book *The Overcomers:*

> "I had to face up to the fact in those stunning losses that God was indeed sovereign; therefore, He was my Lord, my Master, the One in charge of my life, the One who deserved my worship and my service. The road to eternal gain leads inevitably through earthly loss. True faith is operative in the dark. True faith deals with the inexplicable things of life. If we have explanations . . . if things are clear and simple . . . there's not very much need for faith."[6]

This kind of faith is simply trusting Jesus, saying yes to Him for the rest of your life instead of no. Professor George Forell of the University of Iowa says, "Telling a person to have faith is like commanding an insomniac to go to sleep. The harder an insomniac tries to sleep, the more elusive sleep becomes. Faith cannot be commanded any more than sleep. We speak of 'falling asleep'; it is a passive act. Sleep comes as we let go and cease struggling." Likewise, "Faith is created within us when God shows his faithfulness to us."[7]

Fresh encounters with God produce operative faith. Meeting God in new places, seeing Him from a different perspective, and witnessing His fresh power in our lives keeps faith current and alive. This type of faith will never be relegated to the back burner or become an idealized historical statistic.

Stagnant faith, on the other hand, produces frustration. I am reminded of a prisoner in the Bastille in *A Tale of Two Cities,* written by Charles Dickens. The pitiful soul lived for so long in a narrow, dark, monotonous cell cobbling shoes that when he was finally liberated, he went home, and in the center of his house built a similar cell. He had not only grown accustomed to his imprisonment, but he had actually become comfortable with its limitations.

Christians experience a similar imprisonment when they refuse to grow in faith. Growth sometimes involves pain, and a normal human response is to avoid painful experiences. Yet often there is purpose in pain. In pain Paul prayed three times that God would remove his "thorn in the flesh," but God's reply was, "My grace is sufficient for you, for [My] power is perfected in [your] weakness" (2 Cor. 12:9).

Paul's response was not to withdraw and isolate himself from the pain, but to move forward in spite of it. Not fully understanding, but realizing that in God's ultimate plan, his pain had purpose. "Therefore," he said, "I am well content with weaknesses, with insults, with distresses, with persecutions, with difficulties, for Christ's sake; for when I am weak, then I am strong" (2 Cor. 12:10). No inner cell of isolation for Paul—and no frustration with the Father. Because as Christ did His work through Paul, in spite of his weakness, Paul experienced the power of God in his life. And he grew in faith.

Rejection of Previously Held Religious Beliefs

If we are unwilling to acknowledge purpose in pain, we may become alienated from God and reject previously held religious beliefs. During this fourth stage of suffering, the Christian will either abandon what he perceives to be a one-sided fellowship, or he will realize that God is God and ultimately in control of life.

This fourth stage in dealing with crisis is perhaps the most difficult because it is usually ushered in by long periods of silence on God's part. The pit would not be so foreboding, the valley not nearly so deep, if in that pit, in that valley, we could even vaguely detect the presence of the Almighty moving on our behalf. The problem with the pit and the valley is that our limited human perception is often further clouded by our pain. And even though God has promised never to forsake us, we cannot see Him.

That must have been the way the three Hebrew children, Shadrach, Meshach, and Abed-nego, felt as they were bound and made ready for death in the fiery furnace. Their crime was that they would not prostrate themselves in worship before a pagan altar set up by King Nebuchadnezzar. They, like all believers eventually do, found themselves in the midst of a life-threatening crisis.

How did they handle it? They did not accuse God by chiding Him about the injustice of their situation, although it was unfair. They did not have any unrealistic expectations of God, acknowledging that both deliverance or martyrdom were equally possible in His plan. They merely said, "If it be so, our God whom we serve is able to deliver us from the furnace of blazing fire; and He will deliver us out of your hand, O king. But even if He does not, let it be known to you, O king, that we are not going to serve your gods or worship the golden image that you have set up" (Dan. 3:17–18).

Infuriated by their resolve to maintain allegiance to their unseen God, the king had the furnace heated seven times hotter than usual. Then he had his three prisoners bound so tightly that they had to be carried to the place of execution and literally thrown into the blazing fire. But while watching this ghastly event from his safe spectator's stand, Nebuchadnezzar saw something he did not expect. He got a glimpse of the fourth man in the fire, the One who walks through every fiery trial with His followers. Notice this, for it is important: Nowhere in the third chapter of Daniel does the Bible say that either Shadrach, Meshach, or Abed-nego were able to see the fourth man in the fire or that they were even aware of His presence. *Yet He was there* . . . and fully visible to the king. The fourth man—the One who strengthened, protected, and empowered those who remained faithful in the fire—did not come out. He is still there, ready to walk through the flames and take the heat for us—whether we can see Him or not.

It is hard to walk through the crisis when we cannot see His face, hear His voice, touch His hand. Yet one fact is sure: None of us will escape the fiery furnaces of this life unscathed. Adoniram Judson, the renowned missionary to Burma, endured untold hardships trying to reach the lost for Christ. He was thrown into prison where he suffered incredible mistreatment. There he received wounds from his shackles and chains that left him with ugly scars for the rest of his life. Undaunted, when he was released from prison he requested permission to enter another province where he might continue preaching the gospel of Christ. But the godless ruler denied his request for this reason: "My people are not fools enough to listen to anything a missionary might say, but I fear they might be impressed by your scars and turn to your religion."[8]

In God's economy we must not forget that our pain does have a purpose and our scars can serve the Savior. Ask Joni Eareckson Tada, who, because of an untimely diving accident, is a quadriplegic. In her pain Christ has strengthened her and empowered her to touch and encourage thousands of others who have been handicapped by life. Ask David Ring. Crippled from birth by cerebral palsy, yet in his pain he travels from city to city, preaching the good news of Jesus Christ. Ask Clebe McClary, a dashingly handsome Marine who answered the call of his country in Vietnam. There he was disfigured, losing an eye, an arm, and retaining only partial use of his legs. Yet he still preaches the unsurpassed riches in store for those who faithfully follow Christ Jesus. Ask Gayla Chandler, a young pastor's wife, who discovered a malignant tumor in her breast, endured all the hardships of chemotherapy, and now gives hope and help to other women suffering from cancer. Ask Ronnie Deal, minister of students at Hickory Grove Baptist Church, whose last child was born blind and irreversibly physically and mentally handicapped, but who still faithfully guides other peoples' children to place their faith and trust in Jesus Christ. Ask Dr. Joe Craig and his wife, Margaret, who lost their own little son to leukemia, yet year after year escort hundreds in Jesus' name to remote areas of the world, carrying with them life-giving medicine that will bring healing to other little boys and girls.

The choice is ours. Will we abandon God or cling to His unseen hand? Jesus asked His disciples this same question, "You do not want to go away also, do you?" (John 6:67), after many of His followers had withdrawn. But Simon Peter stood tall and spoke the thoughts of generations of believers when he said, "Lord, to whom shall we go? You have words of eternal life. And we have believed and have come to know that You are the Holy One of God" (John 6:68–69).

The faith that outlasts the crisis is authentic and durable. It is there through thick and thin, through the good times and through the bad. When hard times come, at worst it may shudder, but it does not quit.

Harold Myra tells in his book *Living by God's Surprises* about finding on a card buried on the bottom shelf of a quaint book shop, this verse: "And I said to the man who stood at the gate of the year, 'Give me a light that I may tread safely into the unknown.' And he replied, 'Go out into the darkness and put your hand into the hand of God. That shall be to you better than light and safer than the known way.'"[9]

It is sometimes difficult to reach out to One who seems far removed from the pain, injustice, and moral decay that fill this world. Yet when we look at the cross and the empty tomb, we know that our heavenly Father, too, has suffered. Calvary stands as a magnificent demonstration that, out of the worst of all possible situations, God is able to bring salvation and hope and eternal life. Our faith is reasonable. We should hang onto it, cherish it, exercise it, and watch it grow strong.

Gaining the Ultimate Victory

The last section of *Battle Fatigue* will help you gain the ultimate victory in life: the victory over sin and its consequence, death. All humans struggle spiritually, for no matter what our religious persuasion, we are all spiritual in nature. Some satisfy that spiritual nature with Buddha; some, Mohammed; and some, Hare Krishna. Others imbibe a New Age philosophy, complete with crystals, channelers, and movie stars to give it credibility. Humanity seems to be constantly searching for something spiritually authentic, something or someone to fill the void, something or someone with the power to change their circumstances and change them.

Jack Gulledge, former editor of *Mature Living*, tells a wonderful story about Harry Hopkins, personal assistant to President Franklin Roosevelt. Hopkins accompanied Roosevelt as he met with Winston Churchill and Joseph Stalin in the 1945 meeting at Yalta. During a lull, Hopkins asked the three most powerful men in the world if they would sign their autographs for his small son back in the States. They heartily agreed, but the only scrap of paper they could find at that moment was a one-ruble note.

In 1987 that note, worth approximately eight dollars when it was signed, was sold at auction for $42,000. It is the only known document bearing the names of these three men who changed the course of world history. But there is a name of far greater value. This name has influenced history more than any other. The angel announced to Joseph, "You shall call His name Jesus, for it is He who will save His people from their sins" (Matt. 1:21).[1]

For Christians, Jesus alone has the power of God to affect the spiritual nature inherent within each of us. Jesus became a man, experienced pain, and endured temptations. Jesus, the incarnation of God Himself, breathed the air that He created using the lungs He designed. His feet made prints in the sand along the shores of the Galilee; His breath left a vapor in the cool Judean morning mist; His hands gathered stones along the seashore and made a fire to warm and nourish weary, discouraged fisherman.

No matter what kind of mess we have made out of our lives, we are salvageable. Whatever we have done, whatever our condition, whatever that secret sin that still haunts the recesses of our memory—the fact that Jesus came to us, lived with us, and died for us means God still loves us and He still reaches out to touch us and pull us out of the spiritual doldrums. Nothing we have done in the past has made Him love us less, and nothing we will do in the future could make Him love us more than He does right now.

He alone is able to rebuild the broken altars of our lives and convince us that it is never too late to begin again—with Him. The next two chapters will encourage you to allow Jesus to help you pick up the pieces of your broken life and create a beautiful masterpiece.

NINE

Rebuilding Broken Altars

Half-heartedness consists of
Serving God in such a way as
Not to offend the devil.[1]

That particular winter was severe and icy. A father and his young son made their routine trip to the woodshed, braving the falling snow. While the father chopped wood, the owner of a neighboring farm joined the pair for a bit of small talk. When the father finished splitting the wood, the boy held out his small arms and received an oversized bundle of firewood. Soon he was noticeably shifting back and forth under the weight of the wood as his father continued to pile it on.

"Sonny," the neighbor inquired, "don't you have about all you can carry?"

Trusting his father completely, the boy looked at the man and said, "Sir, my father knows how much I can take."[2]

What does God expect of us? What does it actually mean to labor under the pressure of the cross of Jesus Christ? Does God know how much pressure we can stand? Has God custom designed particular spiritual activities for those who call themselves "Christian?"

What Does God Expect Anyway?

I believe God expects believers, those who have openly professed Jesus as Savior and Lord, to accomplish two tasks.

Be His Witness

The first assignment given by God is established in Acts 1:8. Jesus stood on the Mount of Olives commissioning His followers just before His earthly ministry came to an end and He ascended into the heavens. His parting words were, "You shall be My witnesses both in Jerusalem, and in all Judea and Samaria, and even to the remotest part of the earth."

Those who received Jesus' commission knew He had encompassed the world with His request. Realizing His desire, they began implementing His plan, starting where they were, then moving outward in concentric circles. Today, almost two thousand years later, the whole world is hearing the gospel message of Jesus Christ, and His church is reproducing "spiritual children" into the family of God.

Martin Neimoller, that devoted Christian who spent time in a Nazi concentration camp, was asked to speak at Boston University. Afterward, the media that had been covering the event left in disgust, saying, "He spent all those months in a Nazi concentration camp and all he wants to talk about is Jesus Christ." It is natural and normal for Christians to talk about Jesus. We realize our first responsibility in meeting Christ's expectations is to share the good news about Him with others, reproducing spiritual children.

Minister to Other Believers

Our second assignment is found in 1 Corinthians 12:26, where the apostle Paul encouraged us to minister to one another: "And if one member suffers, all the members suffer with it; if one member is honored, all the members rejoice with it."

In this passage Paul compared the spiritual body of Christ, the church, to a living physical body. If one area of the human body suffers pain, it impacts the other areas of the body. A broken leg will immobilize the physical body and cause discomfort throughout the entire system. Likewise, food benefits the entire system by supplying nourishment and satiating hunger.

So it is in the church. When one person in the body is recognized, promoted, or honored, we, the other members, directly benefit and we should rejoice. When a fellow Christian suffers, sins, or is separated from the body, the entire body of Christ suffers the repercussions and the consequences of that pain. It is therefore our duty as fellow members of the body to fulfill Christ's second expectation, that of administering healing to the one who is so afflicted.

There is a scene in *Winnie the Pooh* that goes like this:

Pooh: "Did you fall into the river, Eeyore?"

Eeyore: "Silly of me, wasn't it?"

Pooh: "Is the river uncomfortable this morning?"

Eeyore: "Well, yes, the dampness you know."

Pooh: "You really ought to be more careful!"

Eeyore: "Thanks for the advice."

Pooh: "I think you're sinking."

Eeyore: "Pooh, if it's not too much trouble, would you mind rescuing me?"[3]

The work of the church is to be out there rescuing people, healing them where they hurt, even before they ask.

There we have it: In two small verses are God's expectations of us. Our labors are to be in the areas of spiritual reproduction and spiritual healing. Spiritual reproduction targets those who do not know Christ as Savior. Spiritual healing helps those who are also "laboring under the pressure of the cross" alongside you.

Salt and Light

Interestingly enough, Jesus described His followers as salt, which is a seasoning and preservative for food, and light, which penetrates and dispels darkness (see Matt. 5:13–14).

Imagine what would happen in Christendom if every believer in Christ became what we are called to be—both salt and light. Spiritual salt aptly sprinkled on the world is a change agent, enticing people to come to Christ. Spiritual salt in the lives of believers acts as a preservative, fostering discipleship and growth in the lives of those who profess Him as Lord. Spiritual light in the lives of believers dispels the darkness of sin, provides a well-lit path to God, and gives direction for living the Christian life.

So why is it that Christians cease to be salt and light? I believe it is because they become fatigued as they labor under the pressure of the cross. In the flesh it is impossible. Sometimes we get discouraged when we realize that the accolades are not coming, the hard work is not being recognized, and the long hours are not being properly remunerated. During those times we think of giving up and serving a different master. When we begin to think this way, we become totally unproductive and fruitless in the kingdom of God.

There Is an Alarm Going Off

Throughout the ages God has searched the earth for people willing to become spiritual salt and light. He probes the planet seeking people who don't mind getting their hands dirty cultivating the soil of human hearts, removing the thorns from torn lives, plowing the hard ground of the soul, planting the seeds of His word, watering the tender shoots, remaining with the crops until harvest is complete.

There was such a man in Israel in 860 B.C., a man whose very being seemed composed of salt and light. Elijah, whose name meant "Yahweh is God," was a man confident of the presence and power of God in his life. His nation, once ruled by King David and then King Solomon, had been divided into two kingdoms and was now ruled by two different kings. The Northern Kingdom, Israel, where Elijah lived, was governed by Ahab and his idol-worshiping bride, Jezebel. Together they had launched an unparalleled era of wickedness and idolatry onto a land and a people that had once proclaimed, "Hear, O Israel! The Lord is our God, the Lord is one! And you shall love the Lord your God with all your heart and with all your soul and with all your might" (Deut. 6:4–5). The people had once agreed with God when He admonished them, "You shall have no other gods before Me. You shall not make for yourself an idol. . . . You shall not worship them or serve them; for I, the Lord your God, am a jealous God" (Ex. 20:3–5).

But now morality was at an all-time low. The absolutes of right and wrong had sunk into a quagmire of gray areas and situational ethics. Law and order were vanishing from the land as cultic temple prostitutes lulled the Israelites to sleep on disease-ridden beds of promiscuous sexual activity. The government was corrupt; the people were powerless and lethargic.

Just the other day I was preparing to step outside my house and get the morning paper. It was still very early as I walked to my back door, unbolted the lock, and proceeded to open the door. Instantly, I heard the piercing sound of my alarm system blaring throughout my sleeping neighborhood. In my hurry to get the paper I had forgotten to deactivate the system that had protected my family throughout the night hours.

According to 1 Kings, that is just what had happened in Israel. That nation had experienced the protection and blessings of God for generation after generation. He had been quietly at work in their lives for so long that they gradually began to take His provisions for granted. They ignored His commandments, overlooked His holiness, and neglected His worship. Then one day it stopped raining, His blessings ceased, His protection ended, and all Israel heard an alarm going off. God finally had their attention.

Is there an alarm going off in your life? In your home? In your nation? Moving away from God is a process. No Christian deliberately wakes up one morning and heads his life in a direction contrary to God's leading. No, it happens gradually, a step at a time.

Steps Toward Alienation from God

First, we neglect the quiet times, those intimate moments of fellowship with God and His creation. These times of prayer and Bible study authenticate His presence in our lives.

Next, worship takes second place to weekends. Keeping the Sabbath holy, attending church with the family, studying the Word of God with fellow believers give way to rest, recreational time, or rushing to complete the tasks left undone from the previous hectic week. God's house becomes a hollow place rather than a hallowed place. His people seem prudish rather than pious, and His commandments become commonplace and conventional rather than extraordinary and life-changing.

Third, we find temptation and sin getting a stranglehold on life. Often seemingly committed Christian men and women digress to this dangerous level. Out from under the disciplines and instructions offered by the Word of God and the church, we perceive ourselves accountable to no higher authority. We become our own higher authority and the rule becomes "satisfy the desires of the flesh," or do whatever makes you feel good. That is why, almost on a weekly basis, we hear of another Christian "superstar" who has fallen.

Horatius Bonar expressed it well when he said, "I know that charity covereth a multitude of sins, but it does not call evil good because a good man has done it. It does not excuse inconsistency because the inconsistent brother has a high name and a fervent spirit. Crookedness and worldliness are still crookedness and worldliness, though exhibited in one who seems to have reached no common height of attainment."[4] To move out from under the protective umbrella of God's standards inevitably forces human beings to create a new set of standards that are always inferior to God's. Living under our standards rather than God's opens up a Pandora's box filled with pride, lying, cheating, adultery, drug abuse, and idolatry.

Fourth, we find ourselves at the level of idolatry. In each of us is a God-vacuum that needs to be filled. When we ignore, disregard, and neglect the one true, living God, a gigantic hole in our psyche begs to be filled. So we replace God with gods, worshiping whatever conveniently fills the vacuum. It could be the god of prosperity, the god of success, the god of sexual promiscuity, the god of drugs or alcohol abuse, or perhaps one of the many New Age spirit gods. In any case, when God's people sink to this level of apostasy, it makes God sick, and an alarm goes off in heaven and on earth as He begins the process of getting our attention.

It has been truthfully said, "As goes the individual citizen, so goes the nation." If there is an alarm going off in our individual lives, then we need only to direct our attention north, south, east, and west to hear the blare of chaos across our "Christian" nation. If God is no longer revered and honored in our homes, can we expect Him to be welcomed in our schools? If His name is reviled and His power profaned on prime-time American television, dare we expect more in the halls of Congress? While we condone homosexuality as an acceptable lifestyle for raising the next generation, we silently slip into abortion clinics and bloody our nation's hands under the guise of population control.

As a nation, we have moved far from God and are now staggering under the burdensome weight of our sin. God is sending out a clear alarm; it sounds like social chaos in our streets, economic disaster in the stock market, natural calamities of unsurpassed proportion, and global unrest and uncertainty. Without a doubt, He knows how to get our attention.

First the Fire, Then the Rain

The same scenario occurred in Israel during Elijah's ministry. That nation had moved so far from God that idol worship, Baalism, was commonly practiced, becoming the state religion under Ahab (see 1 Kings 16:31). Baal was worshiped as the god who provided fertility, and it was commonly thought that he manifested himself in thunderstorms.

It is evident that God sets off alarms in nations and in individual lives to direct the focus of His children away from artificial gods back to Himself. In Israel an alarm had been increasingly sounding for three-and-one-half years. In order to get the peoples' attention refocused, God had withheld the rain (see 1 Kings 17:1). When rivers dwindle to streams, when crops wilt in the fields, when animals become parched and dehydrated, when youngsters cry out in the streets for a cool drink of water and a hot piece of bread—believers look toward the heavens for help.

But in Israel they had not looked far enough. They had depended on Baal, the one who supposedly manifested himself in the thunderstorm, the one who promised fertility and ample crops. Yet the skies had been strangely silent for three-and-one-half years. There had been no thunderstorms. There had been no crops. Jehovah God had seen to that.

God knew that Israel had a great physical need for rain, and He was ready to satisfy that craving. But He also identified their greater spiritual need, recognition of His authority as God. To return to God they would have to abandon the loathsome practice of idol worship.

To help His people recognize the difference between gods of stone and Himself, Jehovah set up a contest between His prophet Elijah and the 450 false prophets of Baal plus the 400 prophets of the Asherah, Baal's imaginary wife. They met at Mount Carmel, near the Mediterranean coast of Palestine. There the children of Israel gathered to answer this question, mouthed by Elijah, but inevitably asked by God, "How long will you hesitate between two opinions? If the LORD is God, follow Him; but if Baal, follow him" (1 Kings 18:21).

The rules of the contest were simple. Each contestant was to place a sacrifice on a prepared altar. Each would call on the name of their god, and the god who answered with fire, would be identified as authentic and worshipped as God (1 Kings 18:24). Neither side could ignite the sacrifice; the fire had to come from heaven, just as the much needed rain would come from heaven. The God who had the power to send the fire would be recognized by the people as the God responsible for sending the rain. After all, logically speaking, only the true and living God could send such a fire to reveal His power and then rain to reveal His blessing. The contest was intended to settle this question in the minds of the people, "Who is the real God, Jehovah or Baal?"

Unleashing the Power of God in Your Life

The priests of Baal ceremoniously prepared an ox and placed the dead carcass on the altar, summoning their god to send fire as proof of his existence. As the day lengthened and Baal did not respond with a manifestation of his power, their fervor intensified. They began to leap about the altar, cutting themselves with swords and lances until their blood mingled with that of the sacrifice.

The Bible says they raved on until the "time of the offering of the evening sacrifice" (1 Kings 18:29), literally from noon till three o'clock in the afternoon. They had all the necessary ingredients for worship: 850 prophets, an altar, a sacrifice, much enthusiasm and fervor, plus faith. Yet, verse 29 ends with these dismal words, "but there was no voice, no one answered, and no one paid attention." Why? Because they had no God, which meant they had no power; consequently, they produced no fire.

Have you ever sensed a "divine power outage" in your own life when God's presence seemed far removed from your situation? Would you categorize your prayers as anemic, now-I-lay-me-down-to-sleep utterances that routinely occur just before your head hits the pillow at night? If so, you are definitely spiritually fatigued, trying to maneuver through the hills and valleys of this life on limited power from an exhaustible source of energy.

There is nothing more frustrating than knowing your need for fuel recognizing the energy source, yet not being able to access it to meet your needs. That happens when we attempt to live the Christian life in our own limited human power. We become fatigued by the battle.

Our heavenly Father knows when we are spiritually dry, in desperate need of the rain of His blessings in our lives. However, before He sends the rain, the fire of His Holy Spirit power must fall on our life. Why? So that we who are blessed by the rain will recognize the Source of the fire and acknowledge Him as the "Blesser."

Accessing the Power of God

How do you access the power of God in your life?

Hear from God

Elijah heard from God on a regular basis because he nurtured a dynamic relationship with God. He was listening when God said there would be no rain for three-and-one-half years, and he was still listening when God announced the upcoming shower. He was confident in God's ability to send the fire because he knew the nature, the heart, and the character of God.

Have you heard from God recently? Do you have that vital relationship with Him that only comes by accepting His Son, Jesus Christ as your Savior and Lord? Do you fellowship with Him regularly, communicating with Him in prayer, listening to Him as He speaks to you through His Word? You will never be able to unleash the power of God apart from accessing God Himself.

Get Rid of the Debris in Your Life

Can you imagine the scene there on Mount Carmel when the prophets of Baal completed their charade? Can you see the debris left by those bizarre idol worshipers? In their exhaustion they carelessly left the tools of their trade laying about on the ground.

It might have been a temptation to use some of that material. But Elijah knew not to build an altar to Jehovah God on a foundation consisting of the paraphernalia of idol worship. His first task was to recognize it as garbage, clean up the area, and get rid of it—a task every believer has to periodically perform.

As Christians, we cannot access God's power in our lives if we are holding onto some bit of Baal. We must remove all false gods from our lives, those things that we thought would bring the rain but could not because they are powerless.

Identifying Bits of Baal in Your Life

-1-

The ambition to achieve fame, success, or glory, no matter what the cost to your spiritual life, is a Baal. It involves replacing God with your own ego and self-will.

-2-

Unholy desires can replace God's will in your life. Ask yourself this question, "What is it that I want that God doesn't want for me?

-3-

Memories of the past can crowd God out of your life and bind you to a certain period of time if you are determined to hold on and not move forward. Once a lady was asked by her friend what she was thinking of that made her look so depressed. She replied that she was thinking about her future. When asked what made the future seem so hopeless, she replied, "My past."

Is there anything in your life that you cannot let go of? Does your mind carry you back to an event and hold you captive there day after day? If you spend too much time and energy there, it can become a Baal.

-4-

Unhealthy relationships can stand between you and God. Be careful with whom you choose to spend your time. There are people in our lives who try to draw us away from our power source, directing us toward a path that leads away from God, not toward Him. Be careful not to let unhealthy relationships become a Baal.

-5-

Business activities, as well as recreational endeavors, can draw Christians away from God. It has been well said, "We worship our work, we work at our play, and we play at our worship." If we expend more energy making a living and entertaining ourselves than building a relationship with God, we have created a Baal in our lives.

Remember, anything in our lives that becomes more important than God or pulls us away from God is a Baal and makes us guilty of the sin of idolatry. When Christians recognize the potential for replacing God with Baals, they must take steps to rid their lives of the debris, change direction, put God back on the throne of their lives where He belongs, and faithfully continue their walk with Him.

Repair the Broken Altar

Elijah knew that unused altars deteriorated. He had probably watched as enemies of the Lord deliberately knocked down the stones to hinder the worship of God. He had seen other altars fall apart because of apathy and indifference on the part of the worshipers. More important matters attracted their attention, so they neglected the altar and its significance for their lives.

With lack of use, the altar eventually succumbed to the forces of nature and fell apart. Altars also deteriorate because of carelessness. The worshiper knows the altar is in place, yet he flippantly approaches the altar too hurriedly and inevitably trips over the stones, knocking them out of their proper order, disrupting the atmosphere for worship.

How is it with your altar, the place where you meet God? Has some enemy come into your life, drawn your attention away from God, and destroyed your altar? Has apathy and indifference on your part caused you to be distracted, leaving your altar unattended? Or perhaps you have become careless, allowing your time alone with God to become a matter of convenience. It is time to do what Elijah did when he "said to all the people, 'Come near to me.' The people came near, and he repaired the altar of the LORD which had been torn down" (1 Kings 18:30).

Elijah drew from the knowledge of God and his past heritage and "took twelve stones according to the number of the tribes of the sons of Jacob, to whom the word of the LORD had come, saying, 'Israel shall be your name'" (1 Kings 18:31). He reminded those apostate Israelites of a time when God established their nation, when He made covenants with them contingent on their remaining faithful to Him. He rekindled in their minds the generations of blessings they had received from God's own hand. And so with the "twelve remembering stones," he proceeded to rebuild the broken, unused altar with the foundation stones of his faith, and he did it "in the name of the LORD" (1 Kings 18:32).

It's time to rebuild our broken altars with the following twelve "remembering stones."

Stone 1: Faith

The first stone in our altar must be faith, our confidence in God to be who He says He is. We must also have faith in His ability to do what He says He will do.

It is said that the impala of Africa can jump ten feet high and cover a distance of over thirty feet. It therefore seems strange that these animals can be held in any enclosure with a three-foot wall around it. You see, these beasts will not jump anywhere if they cannot see where they will land.

The Bible says that faith is the ability to trust that which we cannot see. It frees us from the insignificant enclosures of life that only entrap us.

Stone 2: Belief

The second stone is our belief in Jesus Christ, and our acceptance of His sacrificial death on the cross to redeem us from our sinful nature. It begins with a simple tugging on the heart and ends in total commitment of our lives to Him.

When a young country boy was questioned about his salvation experience, he became flustered and fumbled over some of the details. Doubting his experience to be any more valid than the answers to their difficult questions, the adults at his church dismissed him to leave the room as they pondered the legitimacy of his experience with God.

"Wait a minute," the lad cried out. "The best I can see it, Jesus coming into my heart is a lot like fishing. You can't see the fish or even hear the fish, but you can feel it when it grabs that bait and takes off. I'm not so smart as you folks, but I am smart enough to know when I've been hooked by God."

Stone 3 : The Word of God

Comedian W. C. Fields was reported to be very critical of religion. However, one day he was caught in his dressing room reading the Bible. When asked what he was doing studying the very book he had been so critical of, his reply was, "I'm looking for loopholes."

The Word of God has no loopholes. It is the stone that our altar is built around. In this stone we uncover God's plan for all creation and how we fit into that plan.

Stone 4: Prayer

Prayer is the stone by which we access heaven. It is the vital link connecting the Creator with His creation. No altar is complete without the stone of prayer.

According to Henry Ward Beecher,

> Prayer covers the whole of man's life. There is no thought, feeling, yearning, or desire, however low, trifling, or vulgar we may deem it, which, if it affects our real interest or happiness, we may not lay before God and be sure of His sympathy. His nature is such that our often coming does not tire Him. The whole burden of the whole life of every man may be rolled on to God and not weary Him, though it has wearied the man.[5]

Stone 5: Worship and Praise

This stone takes us into the presence of God and allows us to adore, revere, honor, and esteem Him. Worship and praise permit us to celebrate His majesty and thank Him for His mighty works on our behalf.

A businessman and a Christian missionary were traveling together in Korea when they happened upon a strange sight.

In the field they were approaching was an old man holding the handles of a plow while his young son was pulling the plow through the hard ground.

Amused, the businessman inquired whether that family was too poor to purchase an ox. The missionary answered that only a short time ago the family had indeed owned an ox, but they sold it and gave the proceeds to help build the neighborhood church, knowing they would have to pull the plow themselves in the spring.

"What a sacrifice that must have been," replied the businessman.

"Oh, they do not consider it a sacrifice," said the missionary. "They regretted having only one ox to offer the God who had done so much for them."

Stone 6: Fellowship

Zig Ziglar was telling his son Tom a Bible story:

> "Son, David was really a brave boy to challenge Goliath, wasn't he? He was a lad of seventeen and hadn't even started to shave, while Goliath was a man of war over nine feet tall and weighing over four hundred pounds."
>
> Tom looked up at him and said, "Yes, Dad, David was brave all right. But Goliath was really the brave one." Somewhat startled, Zig Ziglar asked Tom why he figured Goliath was the brave one. He said, "Dad, you've got to understand that Goliath was out there all by himself; David had God with him." [6]

Fellowship allows us to remain in constant communion with our heavenly Father. We need never feel alone or deserted if this stone is laid on our altar.

Stone 7: God's Will

Two country boys were engaged in conversation. One of the boys was robust and muscular; the other frail and underdeveloped for his age.

The smaller lad was admiring the other's strength and impressive physique when he said, "If I were your size, nothin' would frighten me. I'd head for the woods, find me the biggest bear there, and tear him limb from limb."

With that the big fellow grinned and replied, "There's lots of little bears in the woods. Why don't you go after one of them?"

God's will gives us direction for our lives. He does not always send us into the woods to tackle the "big bears" but instead perfectly matches our abilities with His own flawless blueprint. It is our individual plan for an intimate walk with Him. It requires absolute trust and a personal knowledge of His lovingkindness toward us.

Stone 8: Holiness

This stone leads us to God, who is holy. It keeps us from being tempted beyond what we are able to resist. If applied to the altar, holiness keeps our thoughts pure and our actions acceptable before God.

A mother was explaining to her daughter what a Christian should be like. After a lengthy theological discussion on the fruits evident in a life lived for Christ, the mother was shocked to hear her daughter's final question. "Mom," she asked, "have I ever met anyone who was a Christian?"

Holy living sets the Christian apart from the rest of the world. If your altar is built around holiness, there won't be any doubt about your authenticity.

Stone 9: Faithfulness

Faithfulness produces the power to hang in there no matter how tough the going gets. Flannery O'Conner said, "What people don't realize is how much religion costs. They think faith is a big electric blanket, when of course it is the cross."[7] As Christians we never have the option to lay the cross aside and walk away from it. As God has proven Himself faithful to us on numerous occasions, it is our responsibility to remain faithful to Him. This stone laid on the altar keeps it from wavering from one position to another.

Stone 10: Commitment

With the stone of commitment we pledge our allegiance to the One who always remains faithful to us. Arthur Tonne, in his book *Lent and the Seven Virtues,* tells the following story of a mother and her fifteen-year-old son who were cruelly tortured in China in 1839.

In an attempt to force them to give up their faith, the mother was forced to watch as her son faced death at the hands of tormenters. At one point during the course of their tortures, an official turned to the horrified mother and said: "What a brave mother you, but where is your love for your boy? With one word you could set him free, you could make him rich and happy. But no, with unfeeling eyes you watch him suffer a terrible death."

This was too much for the mother. She shook with emotion and seemed to be weakening when her son noticed and cried out, "Mother, don't cry and don't weaken. Heaven is worth everything."

"O God," she called out, "forgive my momentary weakness. Make me worthy of such a son. . . . Go, my boy, go bravely to death. My heart and my prayers are with you. Soon I will join you in triumph." [8]

This stone, commitment, makes us unyielding in our devotion, unwavering in our dedication, and steadfast in our loyalty toward God.

Stone 11: Service

The stone of service plugs us into the very nature of God. It allows us to respond to His blessings by assisting others. It opens up a channel of good will that results in healing and restoration within the church as well as outside its boundaries.

People who serve are classified by three words, "and then some." They are thoughtful, considerate, and kind toward others, "and then some." They do all that is required of them, "and then some." They are dependable and can be counted on, "and then some." When we serve others, we are, in essence, showing God our gratitude for all He has done for us. We certainly owe Him that, "and then some."

Stone 12: Perseverance

This stone of perseverance gives our altar endurance and permanence. It screams out, "Never give up your faith. Never give up your faith. Never give up your faith." Through many trials this tenacious stone is longsuffering and persistent. It has the capability to carry us till the end.

Our prayer as Christians should not be centered on mere survival, but the courage to persevere.

Place the Sacrifice on the Altar

After the stones of remembrance were in place, Elijah prepared the ox for sacrifice. He cut it into pieces and "laid it on the wood" (1 Kings 18:33). Then he did a strange thing. He soaked it with water, an obvious attempt to quell the doubters who might be in the crowd. There Elijah stood beside a dead, lifeless, wet ox. It had no power, no rights, no hope of burning without an intervention from God.

Everyone's attention turned toward the pitiful sacrifice. Could such an object of disgrace burn for the glory of God? Elijah uttered a prayer, "O LORD, the God of Abraham, Isaac and Israel, today let it be known that Thou art God in Israel" (1 Kings 18:36). Then he stepped out of the way. "Then the fire of the LORD fell, and consumed the burnt offering and the wood and the stones and the dust, and licked up the water that was in the trench" (1 Kings 18:38). And what was the reaction of the people who witnessed this awesome act of God? They fell to the ground, turning their attention from the burning sacrifice and acknowledging Jehovah as God with their voices and by their actions.

You may have been so beaten down by life that you think you are not worth much to God. You look in the mirror of your soul and see a pitiful, powerless, wet sacrifice incapable of burning for the glory of God. However, God wants you to think of yourself as the light bulb in a huge lighthouse. That bulb by itself only casts a feeble glow into the dark, dangerous night on the seashore. But combined with a powerful system of lenses and reflectors that surround the bulb, its light can be seen by ships for miles around.

An individual Christian, dependent on his own power, can make little difference for God in this dark, dangerous world. But when we admit our weakness and plug into His strength, He greatly magnifies our light with a demonstration of His power. The apostle Paul wrote: "I urge you, by the mercies of God, to present your bodies a living and holy sacrifice, acceptable to God which is your spiritual service of worship. And do not be conformed to this world, but be transformed by the renewing of your mind, that you may prove what the will of God is, that which is good and acceptable and perfect."

All God's children are weak and powerless and incapable of serving Him until we climb on the altar of His will for our lives and present ourselves in all our weaknesses as living sacrifices. We have to get our ambitions and selfish desires out of the way and allow Him to apply the fire of the Holy Spirit to our lives, burning away that which has no substance, and incorporating the power to live victoriously for Him. When this happens, we become usable and others will watch us burn for His glory. They will be changed by the fire they see in our lives and will fall down and confess, "The Lord, He is God."

Wait for the Rain of His Blessing

When the fire fell and consumed the sacrifice, God was vindicated, glorified, and worshiped. The bogus Baal was discredited, disgraced, and dishonored. Hastily, the people destroyed all the false prophets and acknowledged Jehovah as their only God.

Then it was time to go home. They had come to see a contest between gods, but now it was over. Discussing the miraculous events of the day, they started to drift down the little trails that had brought them up the steep sides of Mount Carmel. But the drama was not fully played out; they were still thirsty. Could the God who sent the consuming fire and crushed Baal also provide for their individual needs by sending the much-needed rain?

That is when the thunderheads rolled up over the horizon and the ground shook with the force of their power. That is when the lightning was unleashed and the rain began to pour from a sky heavy with "holy" moisture. Then the people clapped their hands and lifted their wet faces toward the ominous sky in praise and thanksgiving, repeating over and over in chorus, "The Lord, He is God. The Lord, He is God."

Now, back to the original question: "What does God expect of you?"

Nothing "but to fear the LORD your God, to walk in all His ways and love Him, and to serve the LORD your God with all your heart and with all your soul, and to keep the LORD's commandments and His statutes which I am commanding you today for your good" (Deut. 10:12–13). Picture yourself as that little child at the beginning of the chapter who stood with empty arms extended toward a loving, trustworthy father, waiting for the load that would fill his arms. Present yourself to your Heavenly Father, an obedient child ready to rebuild the broken altars of your life and ready to do the work He has commissioned you to do.

What does God expect of you? Only all that you are.

T E N

Realizing It Is Never Too Late

Together we stand at life's crossroads,
and view what we think is the end.
But God has a bigger vision,
and He tells us it's only a bend.
For the road goes on and is smoother,
and the "pause in the song" is a "rest."
And the part that's unsung and unfinished
is the sweetest and richest and best.
So rest and relax and grow stronger.
Let go and let God share your load.
Your work is not finished or ended,
You've just come to a "bend in the road."[1]

Kneeling beside her father, a little girl sleepily stammered through the words of her familiar bedtime prayer. "Now I lay me down to sleep. I pray the Lord my soul to keep. If I should die before I live . . . " Hesitating a bit, she realized her mistake, then continued on: "If I should die before I wake, I pray the Lord my soul to take."

In that half-awake state, she stumbled upon a malady that afflicts millions in our world today, that of giving up too soon.

The ultimate tragedy for a Christian is not death. Physical death ushers us into the presence of God, and eternal life continues at its fullest. The ultimate tragedy is when psychological, emotional, or spiritual death precedes physical death. When this happens we literally die before we have lived. The scenario is predictable. Life presses in on all sides causing fatigue. Because of the pressure, many are tempted to give in and spend the final precious years of life merely going through the motions, never realizing the bounteous Christian experience that has been appropriated in Jesus Christ. And this problem is not confined to Christian laypeople. Christian clinical counselor Cliff Parker estimates up to 40 percent of all preachers suffer from serious stress at some point in their careers. Parker works each year with about twenty-five pastors who suffer from significant problems stemming from overwork, underpay, and job insecurity.[2]

But it should not be that way. The Bible tells us that Jesus came so that we might have a lifetime of spiritual vitality and quickness, and might have it "abundantly" (John 10:10).

Christians are supernaturally endowed by Christ with the vitality to live life to its fullest. Contrary to some schools of thought, this does not suggest worldly prosperity, wealth, or carefree living. It does mean that Christians have the God-given ability to face life's unpredictable circumstances with joy. Jesus said, "These things I have spoken to you, that My joy may be in you, and that your joy may be made full" (John 15:11). This joy is contrasted with weeping and sorrow when Jesus says, "Truly, truly, I say to you, that you will weep and lament . . . but your sorrow will be turned to joy" (John 16:20).

Circumstances sometimes cause weeping, sorrow, even a certain fatigue with living. But the joy of the believer rests in God Himself. He is the ground and object of joy throughout both the Old and New Testaments. With the hope we possess in Christ Jesus when He said, " I will see you again, and your heart will rejoice, and no one takes your joy away from you" (John 16:22), we can face life's eventualities, no matter how traumatic.

If that's the case, then why are there so many down-and-out believers, people who seem to be hanging on to their faith but who have lost their sense of joy in living the Christian life? I believe the problem is clearly recognizable as a chronic case of battle fatigue, and diagnosed by such symptoms as boredom, indifference, lethargy, sluggishness, and the inability to muster the strength to get up and face the repetitiveness of life. Whether caused by physical overextension or continual emotional drains, this "burn-out disorder" is serious because, if left untreated, it causes those who are so afflicted to entertain thoughts of giving up.

An awkward young boy was doing his best to learn to ice skate. He had fallen so many times that in some places on his face the blood and tears ran together. Seeing the lad's plight, a kind gentleman approached the child, picked him up, and compassionately offered this suggestion: "Son, why don't you quit? I'm afraid you are going to kill yourself!"

Brushing the tears from his eyes, the boy thanked his benefactor, but said resolutely, "Sir, I didn't buy these skates to learn how to quit. I bought them to learn how to skate."

Why do people choose to follow Christ and then quit? Is the choice made with the hope that Jesus will act as a vaccine, granting immunity to those who wish to avoid the cuts and bruises on the treacherous ice of life? If so, they have a false perception of who He is and how He operates in the lives of His followers. Jesus is not our hedge against life; He is the infrastructure of our lives. He girds up our wounds and gives us that gentle nudge that pushes us back on the ice, back into life and living, even when we're covered with blood and tears.

Hemingway said, "The world breaks everyone, then some become strong at the broken places."[3] The scars of broken places appear in each of our lives. I once heard a story about a place where priceless urns are produced and then purposely shattered. Using gold and silver as a glue they are reassembled, becoming infinitely more beautiful than in their original, unbroken state. Like the extra fortification and strength found in the area of a mended bone fracture, a broken life repaired and fortified by the gold and silver threads in the Savior's gentle hands becomes a priceless treasure in the kingdom of God. Sometimes, though, in our broken state we do not sense the divine Doctor at work and we concentrate on our brokenness, thinking all is lost. But when Jesus is involved in a life, it is never too late.

When Is It Over?

According to that great American philosopher, Yogi Berra, "It ain't over till it's over." As a high school athlete, I learned that Yogi is right. Winners can exchange places with losers even as the final buzzer sounds and the fans are already filing from the stands. Games have a way of reversing themselves quickly; one extra point finding its way through the goalpost, one three-pointer that lands dead center through the basket, one fly ball that barely makes it over the wall changes losers into winners and vice versa.

Interestingly enough, that profound revelation from the lips of one of baseball's greats is even more applicable to life than to baseball.

The lives of "everyday" Christians are described not by exclamation points, but by commas. They do not make any special claims about themselves spiritually except that Jesus lives in them. They try to do what is right by God and country; they live morally and pay taxes. They serve as deacons and tithe out of their monthly paychecks. They have all the education that restricted resources and limited time will allow. They marry their first real love and raise kids, although not always successfully. They attend the small churches, the ones who struggle to make ends meet, the ones who never have enough people willing to teach Sunday School or work in the nursery. Then retirement and the struggle in the game of life continues; sometimes it even intensifies. Is there any wonder they seem tired and breathless and fatigued, questioning whether or not God has any use for them?

My ancestry goes back to people just like them—no superstars, just common people who sometimes wondered if life might have passed them by and God might have overlooked them. But He hadn't.

Saved during the great Sandy Creek Revival under the preaching of Shubal Stearns, my great-great grandfather, William Farthing, migrated to the mountains of Watauga County. There in North Carolina he patiently farmed a rocky piece of earth by day, and according to my maternal grandmother, "Preached mightily, the redeeming grace of Jesus Christ, by night." Deep in the heart of his wife, my great-great grandmother Farthing, God planted the desire to pray for an offspring who would carry on Grandfather's legacy and preach the gospel. Assuming that offspring would be her son, she began to pray for a child. While God did give her sons, none of them turned out to be preachers. And she died, not having her hope fulfilled.

This simple mountain woman passed her passion for a preacher offspring on to her daughter, my great-grandmother Rebecca Farthing. Rebecca, who married Joseph Cook, migrated to the mountains of Virginia, where they also worked a small farm and raised a family. Rebecca, too, longed for a son who would follow in his grandfather's footsteps and preach, but even though she gave birth to five strong sons, none were preachers.

Great-grandmother Rebecca died unexpectedly, leaving a fifteen-year-old daughter to raise her youthful family. Yet before her death, she too passed along the generational legacy to that fifteen-year-old girl, my grandmother, Edith Widener, who began praying for a preacher son. Still, God remained silent; none of my uncles became preachers.

As a young girl, my mother, Bernice Brown, also prayed for a son who would enter the ministry. When my older brother was born, the family had high hopes that he was the long-prayed-for preacher, but he went in a different direction. God had a surprise. After generations of prayers from the lips of godly women, God made what seemed to be the least likely choice, and chose me.

Early in my ministry, my grandmother stretched as far as she could on her tiptoes, extending her five-foot frame to look at me with piercing crystal blue eyes and gave me a holy charge. "You are the answer to four generations of mothers' prayers. God has finally given us a preacher. Now do what He has called you to do. Preach!"

It is never too late, and you are never insignificant in God's sight! J. A. Holmes once said, "Never tell anyone 'It' can't be done . . . God may have been waiting for centuries for somebody ignorant enough of the impossible to do that very thing.[4] Whoever you are, whatever your age, whatever your condition, God can still make something beautiful of your life. That is His passion, and He is good at it. Whatever you are praying for—even if you have not seen that prayer answered—keep praying. Whatever God has called you to do—even if it seems impossible for you to accomplish it—keep striving. Whatever God has allowed you to dream—even if the dream has not yet been fulfilled—keep dreaming. Whoever God has called you to be, allow Him in His infinite wisdom to fashion you into that person.

Conforming to Christ's Image

What Christians would rather avoid is the conforming process. Yet Romans 8:29 clearly states that the destiny of the elect is to be conformed to the image of Christ. Since Christ no longer inhabits a physical body, this conformity is to His glorious spiritual likeness, His attitude. The apostle Paul wrote, "Have this attitude in yourselves which was also in

Christ Jesus" (Phil. 2:5). The pain in that conformity comes because we are so far removed from the spirit, the nature, the character, the attitude of Christ, that the process of "becoming like Him" is arduous.

Even the patriarchs of old struggled with the process of conformity. Look at strong-willed, irreverent Jacob, father of the twelve ancestors of the twelve tribes of Israel. His very name means, "he cheats, supplants." And throughout the better part of his life he managed very well to live up to that name while his sinful nature struggled against the man God was making of him. His life, a series of conflicts, resulted from the fact that he was rebellious and self-serving. Significant also were his character flaws, those of habitually lying and cheating. These attributes caused him to always be running from someone or something, that is until he ran smack dab into God and began God's conforming process.

Jacob's story occupies nearly half the Book of Genesis. In it we find him cheating his brother, Esau, out of his rightful birthright; lying to and manipulating his blind father, Isaac; leaving home to avoid death at the hands of his brother; being tricked as well as tricking his father-in-law, Laban; and then running for his life again.

Yet the large amount of Scripture appropriated to Jacob's life is not given us so that we might dwell on his shortcomings. His life is truly a chilling exhibit of God's disciplinary action and conformity by affliction in the life of a stubborn human being. Not one of his treacheries went unnoticed by God or unpunished. Even in his golden years the fruits of his life of deception came back to torture Jacob through his children.

For our purposes we want to look at Jacob's personal encounters with God and the way in which those events changed his direction and allowed him to start over. Genesis 28:10–22 is a short, one-night sketch from Jacob's life. As Jacob was fleeing from home and heading toward unfamiliar relatives, God appeared to him at Bethel in his moment of greatest need. Up to this point in his life, this forty-year-old man had merely heard about God's actions in the lives of his ancestors, but he had never had a personal, firsthand experience with Him. Prior to this experience he had depended on his mother's cleverness or his own craftiness to get him through, but now he was alone in the dark. No mother was coming to the rescue. This time he realized that his craftiness had backfired, and as God intervened into his world, Jacob was running for his life.

That night, in a dream, with a stone for a pillow, Jacob watched as angels introduced him to God. There at Bethel, they made a covenant together: God personalized His blessings for Jacob, and in response Jacob worshiped God and vowed to serve Him. That is the first step toward being "conformed to the image of Christ." No one becomes like Christ apart from meeting Him in a personal way. Just as Jacob discovered His nature, His character, and His promises that dark night at Bethel, we too must discover who He is and what He stands for before we can emulate those characteristics in our own lives. Fortunately, it is not necessary to wait for a dream in order for God to be revealed in our lives. His Word fully discloses who He is. We have but to read it to discover God.

On another occasion Jacob was again on the move, headed toward the promised land and possibly impending death at the hand of his brother, Esau, who waited for him there. Jacob and his family had finally broken ties with his father-in-law, Laban. He was truly on his own, and it was time for Jacob to make the right decisions concerning his future. God knew that, because of added responsibilities, it was also time for Jacob to move to a deeper level of maturity.

Genesis 32:24–32 highlights another face-to-face encounter with God that took place at Peniel. There Jacob alone met One who wrestled with him until daybreak. The struggle ended only when the Opponent touched the socket of Jacob's thigh, his hip, and dislocated it. Jacob, however, held on to his Adversary until morning, when he demanded a blessing before release. This was not given until Jacob openly spoke his own name, acknowledging his defeat at the hands of the Stranger, and once and for all revealing his dubious character before God. At that point his Opponent proved His superiority by changing Jacob's name from "cheater," and instead called him Israel, meaning "one on whose behalf God strives."

During this encounter Jacob recognized his weakness before God and learned to depend on Him more fully. Wounded in body but strengthened in faith, he was ready to give God control of his tomorrows. God had taught him obedience through struggling and suffering.

Sometimes God also allows us, totally spent, wounded, and fatigued, to come to the end of our human resources. At that point He demonstrates His unlimited power in our lives, not simply as a superhero to the rescue, but as One intent on conforming us to the image of His Son.

Our Undivided Attention

Jacob finally came to the end of himself at Bethel, and it was there that God was able to get his attention for the first time. In order for God to begin the conforming process in our lives, we have to stop running, realize our own inadequacy, and focus our attention totally on Him. Sometimes this only happens when He patiently steps back and permits us to plot our own route and run the course, realizing in the end that we are no closer to our goals than when we first began the run. It is then, when we are ready to quit, that God reintroduces Himself to us and we will listen.

This has happened in my own life many times. Called to preach as a teenager, I started out as a "flame" for God—and then went to college and somehow misplaced my enthusiasm for ministry. Somehow I had forgotten my grandmother's godly admonition, "Take heed to the ministry which you have received in the Lord, that you may fulfill it" (Col. 4:17). I decided, on my own, that law was my chosen profession. I knew more than God in those early years so I changed my major and set my course for law school. But God was still present in my life. As with Jacob, He had stepped back, waiting for me to stop running and to listen.

In the spring of 1970, I graduated from college. I was also to have entered law school, but a national draft lottery was held to solicit young men throughout the country for service in the army. This was necessary because of our increasing involvement in the Vietnam War. For some reason when I was making all my life plans, I had not considered the impact that war could possibly make on my life; so rather flippantly, along with my buddies in the dorm, we sat down to watch the outcome of the lottery. Never having won anything of significance in my life, I relaxed and settled into the party atmosphere that soon surrounded the event. That is, until that stony-faced master of ceremonies reached into that tumbling drum ten minutes into the proceedings and pulled out my birthdate—number 53 out of 365 possible choices.

For a moment I sat there stunned, asking my friends if I had heard correctly, knowing such a low number meant certain induction into the armed forces and possible time in a war zone. The future, which had seemed so promising, became cloudy. Law school was relegated to the back burner as I started considering all my options while God stood back, still patiently waiting for my frenzied activity to slow down.

After some amount of research I determined that the navy, not the army, was the place for me. So I applied to Naval OCS (Officer's Candidate School). Preliminary tests were administered and passed, and I began the process of waiting to hear whether I would be accepted into the program.

However, during those long days of waiting to hear from naval headquarters, I received that much-dreaded draft notice informing me that I was to report to the nearest Army

Induction Center for enlistment. It looked as if time was running out. Things seemed to be unraveling in my life.

On top of that, two days later I received the disappointing news that my application to OCS had been rejected. I was informed that only two applicants could be processed that month from my state, and both had to have minority status; that excluded me. I knew it was over, nothing left to do but join the army and let fate determine the future. That day, like Jacob, I came to the end of myself, stopped running, and reintroduced myself to God, who had been waiting for a long time for me to do just that.

I had not realized it until that point, but God had been at work in my life all along, bringing me to the place where I could develop a listening ear. That night, alone with Him, I was reintroduced to His nature, His character, and His promises for my life. Through His Word, He personalized His blessings to me, and I vowed that He would be my God forever. He had begun that painful process of conforming me to the image of His Son.

I discovered, like a trapeze artist traveling from one high point to another, that I could not reach my destination by holding onto one swinging bar while grasping for another. In life, as on that swinging trapeze, we do not have forever to make up our minds. We must let go in mid air and leap! The process is designed to increase our faith, to teach us that even when we fall, God is there as a spiritual safety net. Our security is not in that swinging bar, whatever that may be; our security is exclusively in God.

The next morning, still disappointed but confident of God's safety net in my life, I started considering plan B, when the telephone rang. To my astonishment, I was informed that one of the two previously chosen officer candidates had declined his appointment to OCS, and I, after it was already too late, was accepted into Naval Officer's Candidate School.

"It ain't over till it's over"—and it is never over when God is involved.

How We Limit Ourselves

Preconceived Inadequacies

Anytime God has accomplished a great work in my life, He has required me to let go and in faith jump closer to Him. That's frightening. Often my spirit is willing, but my flesh, that old selfish, self-serving nature, says, "No way!" I look at myself and then I look at what God has asked me to do, and my preconceived inadequacies become a barrier and cause me to confess, "I can't."

I remember taking my children to the circus when they were small. One of the kids became fascinated with a large elephant who was immobilized in a certain spot by what looked to be an insignificant chain that went from his leg to a small stake in the ground. That stake was not more than ten feet from where he peacefully munched hay.

Curious, I asked his keeper what kept the pachyderm from pulling up the stake and running for the high country. "Perception," he said. "As soon as he was big enough to take away from his mamma, he was staked out there by the entrance gate and given a little hay and water. There he served as a show-stopper when folks came in and went out of the circus grounds. Every once in a while, I'd see the little fellow tug on that chain and pull at the stake with his trunk, but he was small then. No matter how much he tugged, he wasn't big enough to move the stake. Then finally, one day he just quit trying to free himself. The only thing I can figure is that he must have come to the conclusion that the stake was immovable. Now look at him. Big enough to bring the show tent down, but held fast by a stake he could easily pull out of the ground."

Life's "I can'ts" are based on yesterday's "I wasn't able to's." We look at ourselves in light of previous failed performances and are frightened to jump out in faith and trust God to accomplish the impossible through us. Our attitude binds us to one location, one ideology, one insignificant stake.

That is what happened to Gideon. One day the angel of the Lord sat down under an oak tree where Gideon was working and introduced himself by proclaiming, "The LORD is with you, O valiant warrior. . . . Go in this your strength and deliver Israel from the hand of Midian" (Judg. 6:12, 14).

"Me?" Gideon must have answered, pointing to himself. "You can't be talking to me." Now come Gideon's perceived perceptions about himself. "Behold, my family is the least in Manasseh, and I am the youngest in my father's house" (Judg. 6:15). "I'm not adequate for the job. Look at my past history. You'd better find someone else."

Yet in Gideon's case, as in ours, the Lord will not take "I can't" for an answer. His reply to Gideon is the same one we hear when He calls us to some noble, heavenly chore: "You can do it because I will be with you" (see Judg. 6:16). That fact alone assures our success. Our job is to trust Him to help us pull up the stakes that bind us and move forward.

Past Failures

We all have at least one thing in common—the propensity for failure. At some point in life we have fallen short of our own, or even worse, someone else's expectations. You may have failed to hit the home run that could have saved the championship Little League game. Or perhaps you failed the test that could have kept you from repeating that obnoxious calculus class. Maybe you failed to make the cheerleading squad or first chair clarinet in the orchestra. Possibly you even failed to keep a promise to your child or a vow to your spouse.

Whatever that failure, I would venture to guess that you have never forgotten it. Nothing seems to stick with us as vividly as the memory of some past failure. I will never forget the time I ran down the football field anticipating the pass to my side of the line. The spotlight was on me; my best girl was in the stands; the crowd was on its feet cheering; and I stepped in a hole, lost my balance, and let the ball slip right through my hands. It cost my team an important game. Even though that has been nearly thirty years, you would not believe how many times I have rerun that play in my mind.

Dr. Bob Cook, president of King's College, once said, "The secret of succeeding is . . . failing, getting up and acknowledging that you failed, asking forgiveness where you need to, and getting up again and taking another stab at it." That is the real dilemma associated with failure: having the guts to try to do again what we have already failed at once.

Moses faced that dilemma. He knew what God wanted Him to do: liberate the sons and daughters of Israel from slavery in Egypt. His predicament was that he had already tried it and failed. His original plan had been to eliminate one naughty Egyptian at a time, and he had already eliminated the first one. But the plan went haywire, and he had to leave Egypt with a murder charge hanging over his head. He may have left muttering something like, "I wipe my hands of the whole mess. I'd rather be a shepherd in the Sinai and lead sheep than those stubborn Israelites."

And that is just what he was doing forty years later when God appeared to him on a barren mountainside and commissioned him to go back to Egypt and try it again. Moses's reply was, "Who am I, that I should go to Pharaoh, and that I should bring the sons of Israel out of Egypt?" (Ex. 3:11). "Remember me, God? I tried that once and failed. Why, there is probably still a warrant for me in Egypt. You've got the wrong man. It's too late for me to start over. Look at my reputation. Maybe you'd better find someone with a better looking résumé."

But God was not ready to accept "I'm not qualified" as an excuse. He is the great Qualifier, always in the business of preparing us, adapting us perfectly to fit the criteria in His job description.

Gutzon Borglum is the sculptor who is credited with fashioning the stone head of Lincoln that rests in the Capitol in Washington, D.C. When he began the sculpting, he worked with a large square block of stone in his studio. On one occasion, when the face of Lincoln was just becoming recognizable out of the stone, a small child walked through the studio with her parents. Amazed, she asked Borglum if that person in the stone might really be Abraham Lincoln. When he replied yes, she responded in disbelief, "Well, how in the world did you know that he was in that block of stone?" Sometimes, when we look at ourselves, we only see that which represents the present or that which illustrates the past. But when God looks at us, He sees the future and all that we can become in His skilled hands.

When we listen to the voices from our past, we can become confused about what is in our future. We are like the youngster who listened, night after night, as his mother read to him the story of the "Three Little Pigs." He was enthralled, soaking up every minute detail of the fascinating story.

Then, one night his mother decided to read to him from the Bible. She chose Revelation 3:20, which says, "Behold, I stand at the door and knock; if anyone hears My voice and opens the door, I will come in to him, and will dine with him, and he with Me." When the reading was finished, she looked at her son and asked, "If Jesus ever knocks at your heart's door, Tommy, will you open the door and let him in?"

Without blinking an eye, Tommy declared vehemently, "Not by the hair on my chinny-chin-chin."

That may well describe many Christians. God approaches us carrying a huge block of stone, ready to chisel from it a magnificent work of art, a likeness of His precious Son—but all we recognize are the tools that hammer and cut and break apart the rough edges of the stone. They represent the pain associated with becoming like Christ, the pain of conforming to His image. So we step back, away from God, thinking that we have tried to be like Christ before and failed. We say, "I'm tired of struggling to be what You are trying to make of me. Look at my past record. I'll never be qualified!"

If anything similar to that has ever crossed your lips or your mind, then let me offer you a word of encouragement, a sure cure for spiritual battle fatigue:

> As you therefore have received Christ Jesus the Lord, so walk in Him, having been firmly rooted and now being built up in Him and established in your faith, just as you were instructed, and overflowing with gratitude.
>
> See to it that no one takes you captive through philosophy and empty deception, according to the tradition of men, according to the elementary principles of the world, rather than according to Christ
>
> For in Him all the fulness of Deity dwells in bodily form, and in Him you have been made complete, and He is the head over all rule and authority.
>
> — Colossians 2:6–10

If you must harken back to your past, do not dwell on your mistakes; concentrate on the things you did right. You received Christ and committed yourself to a daily walk with Him. That was a right choice. Now, like a pro tennis player who sees the opponent's ball bearing down from the opposite court, you must follow through if you are to win this game. Yes, the sun is bearing down; yes, there are conflicting voices to be heard from the stands; certainly you are facing a formidable foe; but do not dare give up! Your Coach is standing on the sidelines watching your every move, reminding you of the long hours of preparation, planning out workable strategies, giving good advice. Listen to Him. Play in His strength if yours is depleted. Remember, when you are weak, He is strong. "In Him you have been made complete." You are qualified.

Future Perceptions

There was a time not so long ago when no one could have conceived of replacing the horse-drawn buggy with an automobile. Even more farfetched was the concept of flying through the air like a bird. And traveling through space? Why, that notion was simply preposterous. Yet now, when men have walked on the moon, traveling at the speed of sound does not even raise an eyebrow anymore. We have moved far beyond the wildest imaginations of our ancestors because someone somewhere dared to dream.

For many of us, dreaming of what might be is often eclipsed by the fear of what could be. Daring to move beyond the present is, for some, a frightening experience. It is treading on the unknown, walking in the unfamiliar, exercising faith in the God who claims to have His hand on the door to the future. But sometimes we are afraid for Him to open that door. The comfort and the security we perceive to be based in the present often pushes with great force against that door, striving to keep it closed, scaring us with imaginations of what might be on the other side.

Fear is a powerful force in life. Fear keeps the unskilled swimmer from jumping into deep water. It keeps the child, already burned once, from touching the hot stove again. It keeps us a safe distance from the edge of the treacherous mountain cliff. Yet with all its benefits, fear has the propensity to disable the Christian. It can be as dangerous as a poisonous snake whose paralyzing venom engulfs a victim's body, rendering him immovable. Fear keeps its victim from realizing his dreams, robbing him of his hope for the future.

The key to disarming fear in our lives stems from knowing its source. Paralyzing fear does not come from God, according to Proverbs 3:25–26: "Do not be afraid of sudden fear, nor of the onslaught of the wicked when it comes; for the LORD will be your confidence, and will keep your foot from being caught." This fear from Satan incapacitates and will keep us from accomplishing God's plan for our lives. Imbibing this satanic fear tactic will cause us to be afraid of reaching into the future because of our anticipation of failure. This fear of not measuring up to other's expectations may bring with it apprehension of sure punishment.

This is not the same kind of fear associated with Proverbs 1:7, which says, "The fear of the LORD is the beginning of knowledge."

This fear, a reverence for God expressed in our submission to His will, is the starting point and essence of wisdom for the Christian. Wisdom of who God is and His ultimate plan in our lives never incapacitates us; it frees us to expand our horizons and be all that God wants us to be without fearing the future.

Fear of Death

Research proves that human beings fear many things; but the greatest fear is the fear of our own mortality—death. Death seems to be always lurking somewhere, ready to pounce on an unsuspecting victim in an unguarded moment. The time of our appointment is uncertain, as is the where and the how of our meeting, but every living being with a modicum of discernment is sure of one thing: death is inevitable. That somber knowledge, combined with a sense of hopelessness, can cause battle fatigue. Without a proper perspective of our own mortality, the future can be neutralized by thoughts of impending doom and gloom. Dag Hammarskjöld once said, "In the last analysis, it is our conception of death which decides our answers to all the questions life puts to us."

An eat-drink-and-be-merry-for-tomorrow-we-may-die" philosophy has evolved in societies that have no hope beyond their own limited mortality. However, as Christians, even though we often fear the uncertainties surrounding death—the circumstances, the pain, the separation—we are not without hope. Proverbs 14:32 says, "The righteous has a refuge when he dies." Our refuge is "the hope of eternal life, which God, who cannot lie, promised long ages ago" (Titus 1:2). God provided this hope "through Jesus Christ our Savior, that being justified by His grace we might be made heirs according to the hope of eternal life" (Titus 3:6–7). While death seems but a sad end to life, its celestial purpose is to release the Christian to begin life eternal with God. Harold Myra agrees that death is the culmination of a life filled with "God's surprises, and the ultimate surprises are ahead, beyond the grave, where our prayers will become communication face to face."[5]

The thought of dying bothered Jesus, but not the thought of death. When He contemplated the humiliation, the pain, the process, He cried out, "Abba! Father! All things are possible for Thee; remove this cup from Me" (Mark 14:36). Jesus knew His dying not only involved extreme physical suffering but spiritual pain, as the sinless One became sin during the process of redemption. Yet in His supreme hour of distress, He completely yielded His will to God and obediently said, "'My Father, if this cannot pass away unless I drink it, Thy will be done'" (Matt. 26:42).

Death held no fear for Jesus, who deep within its clutches cried out with a loud voice, "'Father, into Thy hands I commit My spirit'" (Luke 23:46). Then with the knowledge that those heavenly hands were ready to receive Him, He breathed His last, and committed His eternal spirit to God, trusting Him for resurrection.

Jesus is both our hope and our proof that it is never too late. Everything we will encounter in life, Jesus has already passed through, preparing our way through His death and resurrection. Thus we too can face our greatest fear with confidence, singing, "O death, where is your victory? O death, where is your sting? Thanks be to God, who gives us the victory through our Lord Jesus Christ" (1 Cor. 15:55, 57).

Christ's resurrection power not only sustains us in death; it also is at work in the lives of Christians. Mark Link noted:

> Each time we love again after having our love rejected, we share in the power of the resurrection. Each time we fail and try again, we share in the resurrection. Each time we hope again after having our hope smashed to pieces, we share in the resurrection. Each time we pick up the pieces, wipe our tears, face the sun, and start again, we share in the power of the resurrection. The message of Easter is that nothing can destroy us anymore—not pain, not sin, not rejection, not death. The message of Easter is that Christ has conquered all, and that we too can conquer all, if we put our faith in him.[6]

John Chrysostom, who lived between A.D. 374 and 407, was brought before the emperor and warned not to preach the gospel of Jesus Christ.

"If you do not give up Christ I will banish you from the country," said the emperor. "You cannot, for the whole world is my Father's land," replied Chrysostom.

"Then I will take away all your property," retorted the emperor. "You cannot, my treasures are in heaven," responded Chrysostom.

"Then I will take you to a place where there is not a friend to speak to you." Chrysostom said, "You cannot. I have a friend who is closer than a brother. I shall have Jesus Christ forever."

"Then," the emperor spewed forth his final threat, "I will take away your life."

"You cannot!" declared Chrysostom triumphantly. "My life is hid with God in Christ." How do you explain a person like that?

A. W. Tozer has attempted it. Tozer says,

> [The Christian] feels supreme love for One whom he has never seen; talks familiarly every day to Someone he cannot hear; expects to go to heaven on the virtue of Another; empties himself in order to be full; admits he is wrong so he can be declared right; goes down in order to get up; is strongest when he is weakest; richest when he is poorest and happiest when he feels the worst. He dies so he can live; forsakes in order to have; gives away so he can keep; sees the invisible, hears the inaudible, and knows that which passeth knowledge.[7]

Athanasius, a great Christian and one of the early church fathers, was asked by a rumormonger, "Don't you know that the Emperor is against you, the bishops are against you, the church is against you, and the whole world is against you?" Confident and fearless, Athanasius replied, "Then, I am against the whole world."

With Christ, you against the whole world is a resounding majority. Do not become fatigued by the "I can't," "I won't," and the "It's not possible" mentality in this world. "You are a chosen race, a royal priesthood, a holy nation, a people for God's own possession" (1 Pet. 2:9). Confess it, stand up against the whole world if necessary, and live it by "proclaiming the excellencies of Him who has called you out of darkness into His marvelous light" (1 Pet. 2:9).

You can be more than you ever dreamed. You can overcome your past. You can move beyond your fears and accomplish the impossible. With God "all things are possible" (Matt. 19:26), and it's never over. It is never too late.

CONCLUSION

Remembering the Best

In a popular children's story, King Fafer had three sons. He wanted to prepare them for ruling his kingdom. So he sent them on expeditions, hoping that, as they explored the world, they would also find wisdom. And indeed, that happened.

While traveling with a caravan, the boys noticed that one of the camels was missing. As they searched for the camel they learned many things. They noticed that he only ate grass on his left side, so they deduced that he must be blind in his right eye. They discovered he must have two teeth missing because he left grass as he grazed. They determined that one of his legs was paralyzed as they followed his distinguishable trail in the sand where he dragged it. To the delight of their wise father, his sons had found knowledge and wisdom while looking for the camel. They had used deductive thinking that he knew would be an asset when they ruled the land.

Sir Horace Walzo, after reading this children's book, coined a new word for the English language based on King Fafer's make-believe kingdom of Serendip. The word coined was *serendipity*.

Serendipity means searching for one thing of value, and in that searching, finding another different treasure of even greater value. Life is a serendipity. Jesus reminds us that our constant search for peace, contentment, happiness, and security must first lead us to Him. Jesus does not simply instruct His followers to listen to His words, although they are extremely important. Rather, He invites them to follow Him, and in following Jesus we discover a path that leads to the peace, purpose, and contentment so desperately sought after in this life.

There is a beautiful illustration of serendipity in the New Testament. As Jesus traveled, He purposefully went through an area called Samaria. There, He was looking for a person who that very day needed Him desperately. He was looking for that person whose life was bankrupt and lonely and mundane, yet salvageable. He purposely stationed Himself by the well in the city of Sycar and waited for what appeared to be a chance meeting with an imperfect stranger.

Then, there she came, down the winding path that criss-crossed that stony hillside. Scripture tells us she was carrying a lot of excess "life baggage" as she walked toward Jesus that day. A social outcast, a misfit, a failure—she had been married many times in a vain attempt to find security, peace, joy, and fulfillment. Now she was living in sin with a man who was not even her husband. Miserable and tortured by the mess she had made of her life, she unknowingly approached the holy Son of God who sat there by the well. She was seeking only to fill the empty water pitcher on her head so that she could quench her physical thirst. Yet her "chance" meeting with a "perfect" stranger turned into fellowship with the Savior who filled her empty life with "living water" and changed her attitude forever.

That, in essence, is the human dilemma. We have been searching for peace, joy, and contentment, all neatly packaged in a box labeled "relationships and things." What we really needed all along was not something to satisfy our wants and desires, but something to fill our empty souls and lonely hearts. Scripture tells us that after this woman openly confessed her life to Jesus and accepted the living water that only He could provide, she was changed forever and left that encounter telling everyone about her newfound friend.

Life is a serendipity. If you seek happiness you may end up being sorrowful, but if you search for God, you will discover the tranquility, the strength, and the power for living that has so eluded you in the past.

Jesus has promised a blessing for all those who desire that which only God can give: complete satisfaction. That is why, in John 7:37, we hear Jesus crying, "If anyone is thirsty, let him come to Me and drink. Whoever believes in Me, as the Scripture has said, from his innermost being shall flow streams of living water." John the apostle does not leave that text for interpretation. He tells us exactly who it is who brings the satisfaction, the wholeness of mind, body, and spirit to the life of the believer. John continues in John 7:39, "But this He spoke of the Spirit, whom those who believed in Him were to receive."

Your greatest need at this moment is to have Jesus touch you as only He can through His Holy Spirit. All you need do is to make yourself available to Him, accepting His power for your life, living in His abundant strength, turning your life completely over to Him, allowing Him to equip you to walk, run, fly.

An observer watching the great Michelangelo work on a statue commented that he seemed to be wasting a lot as he chipped away at the huge block of expensive marble. Michelangelo, the great sculptor, stopped and said, "It is not the chips that fall that count, but the image that appears."

In the same way the Master Sculptor, Jesus Christ, is shaping your life. He has an image of perfection that He wants to produce. He may chisel away some things that seem very important to you. The work of the Sculptor may bring pain to your heart as He chips at the box labeled "things and relationships," so hold on to that box loosely.

You may not be able to change your situation; but just like that woman at the well, you can change your focus from common water and place it on "living water." When you do, your attitude will change and you will never forget what's really necessary for your survival.

The Scottish have a story about a shepherd watching his sheep. He saw an unusual flower on the mountainside, and went closer to look at it more carefully. When he picked the flower, the mountainside mysteriously opened, revealing treasures beyond his imagination inside. Cautiously, he walked in—amazed at the gold, diamonds, and precious stones. Dropping the flower, he frantically filled his pockets with treasure when a little voice said, "Don't forget the best." He ignored the voice and continued his greedy pursuit of the treasures. But the voice persisted. "Don't forget the best," it said. He picked up more treasure and then noticed that the mountain began to close. Hurriedly he ran to reach the mouth of the cave, barely making it just as the mountain closed.

Then from inside the mountain the faint voice called out to him once again, "You forgot the flower. You forgot the best." And the priceless treasure turned to dust.

As opportunities open up allowing you to acquire the riches of this world, "Don't forget the best." The flower that causes your life to bloom is Jesus Christ. He alone offers you the true and lasting treasures of this life, resources that protect you from life's relentless battle fatigue. Listen to the small voice of the Holy Spirit whispering, "Don't forget the best. Don't forget Jesus."

ENDNOTES

PART ONE

1. *Illustration Digest* (Mar./Apr. 1992), 5.

ONE

1. Benjamin R. DeJong, "Wait On," *Uncle Ben's Quotebook,* (Irvine, Calif.: Harvest House Publishers, 1977), 24.

2. George Sweeting, *Great Quotes and Illustrations* (Word, 1985), as found in *The Pastor's Story File* (Nov. 1985), 7.

TWO

1. DeJong, 35.

2. Lloyd John Ogilvie, *A Future and a Hope* (Dallas: Word, 1988).

3. Ibid.

4. *Illustration Digest* (July/Aug. 1992), 3.

THREE

1. DeJong, 304.

2. Ibid., 33.

3. Jamie Buckingham, *Where Eagles Soar* (Lincoln, Va.: Chosen Books, 1980), 45.

4. Ibid.

5. Andrew Murray, *Abide in Christ* (Springdale, Pa.: Whitaker House, 1979), 112.

PART TWO

FOUR

1. DeJong, 130.
2. R. D. Hitchcock, *The Pastor's Story File* (Feb. 1988), 8.
3. Harold Myra, ed., *Leaders* (Waco, Tex.: Word), 61. In *The Pastor's Story File* (Oct. 1988).
4. DeJong, 68.
5. Booker T. Washington, *The Pastor's Story File* (Feb. 1988), 8.
6. Victor Hugo, *The Pastor's Story File* (Oct. 1988), 5.
7. J. Oswald Sanders, *Spiritual Leadership* 37–38, from *The Pastor's Story File* (Oct. 1988), 3.
8. A.W. Tozer, *The Pastor's Story File* (Oct. 1988), 1.

FIVE

1. DeJong, 228.
2. William F. Harley Jr., *His Needs, Her Needs* (Grand Rapids, Mich.: Revell, 1986), 175.
3. Karen Peterson, "Success in Marriage May Be a Matter of Style," *USA Today* (Apr. 4, 1994).
4. Alison Bass, "What Makes a Marriage Fail," *Charlotte Observer* (Dec. 12, 1993).

SIX

1. Byron Frederick, "Ohio Grange Monthly," as cited in *The Pastor's Story File* (1987), 5.
2. *The Pastor's Story File* (1987), 3.
3. Brian Harbour, *Living Abundantly* (Nashville: Broadman Press, 1992), 113.
4. George Sweeting, compiler, *Great Quotes and Illustrations* (Waco, Tex.: Word, 1985). In *The Pastor's Story File* (Nov. 1987).
5. Eleanor Berman, "Further Confessions of an Advertising Man," *Success* (Feb. 1984).
6. Jimmy Carter, *Why Not the Best?* (Nashville: Broadman Press, 1975), 59.
7. George Hodges, *The Pastor's Story File* (Feb. 1988), 8.
8. J. Hudson Taylor, *Uncle Ben's Quotebook*, 98.
9. Denis Waitley and Reni L. Will, *The Joy of Working* (New York: Dodd Mead & Company, 1985), 253.
10. Harbour, *Living Abundantly*, 111.
11. Dr. Victor Frankl, from George Sweeting, *Great Quotes & Illustrations* (Waco, Tex.: Word, 1985), *The Pastor's Story File* (Sept. 1988), 1.

12. Ross West, *How to Be Happy in the Job You Sometimes Can't Stand* (Nashville: Broadman, 1990), 80–86.

13. J. Emmett Henderson, "Christian Ideals and Economic Realities," *Pulpit Digest* (Sept./Oct. 1976), 6.

14. Elie Wiesel, *Messengers of God* (New York: Random House, 1976), 26–27. Also found in *The Pastor's Story File* (Sept. 1988), 3.

SEVEN

1. DeJong, 180.

2. Alexander Solzhenitsyn, *The Pastor's Story File* (Sept. 1988), 5.

EIGHT

1. DeJong, 260.

2. Letter used by permission; name withheld by request.

3. Harold Myra, *Living by God's Surprises* (Waco, Tex.: Word), 23. In *The Pastor's Story File* (Aug. 1988).

4. Creath Davis, *Lord, If I Ever Needed You It's Now, The Pastor's Story File* (Mar. 1988).

5. Myra, 23.

6. Russell Chandler, *The Overcomers* (Old Tappan, N.J.: Revell, 1978), 15–16.

7. Keith E. Krebs, "Double Minded" in George Forell, *Amazing Grace: Six Studies in Galatians,* as cited in *The Pastor's Story File* (Apr. 1988), 6.

8. Courtney Anderson, *To the Golden Shore* (Boston: Little, Brown and Company, 1956), *The Pastor's Story File* (Aug. 1988).

9. Myra, 67–68.

PART THREE

1. Jack Gulledge, *Mature Living*, as cited in *Illustration Digest,* (Nov./Dec. 1989), 9.

NINE

1. DeJong, 205.

2. Gary L. Carver, *Preaching* (Sept./Oct. 1990), 42.

3. A. A.Milne, *Winnie-the-Pooh. The Pastor's Story File* (Aug. 1991).

4. Ralph Colas, "Horatius Bonar," in *Baptist Bulletin* (May 1976) as cited in *The Pastor's Story File* (Feb. 1992), 6.

5. *The Pastor's Story File* (May 1989), 7.

6. Zig Ziglar, "Sunday Sermons," Nov.-Dec., 1983, copied from *The Pastor's Story File* (Feb. 1989), theme: spiritual discipline I, vol. 5, no. 4, p. 8.

7. Flannery O'Conner, *The Pastor's Story File* (Feb. 1989), 7.

8. Arthur Tonne, *Lent and the Seven Virtues* (Emporia, Kan.: Didde Printing, 1956), 50.

TEN

1. *The Pastor's Story File* (May 1988), 6.

2. "Pastoral Stress," *Charlotte Observer* (July 12, 1994), 1A, 4A.

3. Ernest Hemingway as cited in *The Pastor's Story File* (May 1988), 2.

4. J. A. Holmes, *Parables, Etc.* (Feb. 1984), vol. 3, no. 12, p. 8.

5. Harold Myra, *Living by God's Surprises*, 153.

6. Mark Link, *Illustrated Sunday Homilies*, Year B, Series 1, as cited in *The Pastor's Story File* (March 1992), 6.

7. A.W. Tozer, *Parables, Etc.* (Feb. 1984), 4.